My
(*not so*)
Storybook Life

A Tale of Friendship and Faith

ELIZABETH OWEN

Guilford, Connecticut
An imprint of Globe Pequot Press

skirt!® is an attitude . . . spirited, independent, outpoken, serious, playful and irreverent, sometimes controversial, always passionate.

Text design: Sheryl P. Kober
Layout: Kirsten Livingston
Project editor: Kristen Mellitt

Library of Congress Cataloging-in-Publication Data is available on file.

ISBN 978-0-7627-7357-2

Printed in the United States of America

10 9 8 7 6 5 4 3 2 1

Contents

This book is 99.9 percent true. The other 0.1 percent is embellished for comic effect with the express purpose of causing you to laugh, snort iced tea up your nose, and forget for a few hours that your laundry room looks like the aftermath of Mount St. Helens and the children in the backyard are turning your herb garden into a mud-wrestling pit.

You're welcome.

Prologue

Anne reclined by the bubbling brook, twirling a loose string on the red-and-pink patchwork quilt beneath her. The bright yellow Canadian summer sun glowed above her, the birds chirping in the nearby lush woods, the breezy air rustling her long red curls.

"Gil, can we start house hunting soon?"

"Sure." Gilbert leaned back on his elbows and took a big bite of a ripe apple. "I've been thinking it might be time for us to leave Prince Edward Island. Stretch our wings a bit. Start life, our life, together somewhere new."

Anne sat upright. "What? We've never talked about leaving the island!"

"Yeah, I've just been mulling it over . . ." Gilbert took another big bite as a dove cooed in the nearby bushes.

"But I love this place!" Anne brushed her fiery hair out of her face. "What about the farmhouse down on Hummingbird Cove? The one with the hundred-year-old roses on the porch! I thought we were going to fix it up, add on a bigger kitchen? Make it look just like Green Gables?"

"Oh, Annie." Gilbert made a sour face. "That old termite trap? Look at this brochure I picked up. I think you'll be really excited."

Anne reached out and took the brochure, eyeing it as cautiously as Marilla eyed Yankee tourists. "Lakeview Terrace?"

"That's where we're moving." Gilbert's eyes twinkled. "We're going to leave all these country hicks behind and start

over. In the city! Did you know they have ten different floor plans to choose from? And all the houses are a new style; they call them 'ranch' homes. Isn't that exciting?"

"Not really," Anne muttered darkly.

"And the best thing is they have an elementary school, post office, church, and grocery store all right around the corner. They're calling these places 'subdivisions.'"

"No!" Anne slammed the brochure into the dirt. "I want the country! I love nature and birds and starry nights! I want my farmhouse on Hummingbird Cove!"

"Let's be reasonable." Gilbert patted her hand. He knew Anne's emotional temper could quickly spiral into a sparkling fire ablaze with unladylike adjectives and punches thrown from the shoulder. His only defense was distraction. "Are you hungry? Let's go get you some food. How about a chocolate shake? Or one of those mint sundaes you like so much at the drugstore?"

Anne frowned and pursed her lips, allowing Gilbert to help her up off the ground. "But Gil . . . I have really always wanted that farmhouse . . ."

"Shhhh, you'll feel better once you've eaten something."

Anne found herself being led from the meadow, pictures of mint sundaes dancing in her head, the farmhouse on Hummingbird Cove waving from the distance in her memory. She didn't know it then, but she was destined to downsize Marilla's antique furniture to small modern sleeper sofas and sell the family china because it couldn't be washed in the dishwasher Gil bought from Sears and Roebuck. It was the beginning of the end. The end of well water and crickets and dusty summer roads.

It was the end of country life and girlish fantasies. It was the beginning of lawn mowers, mosquito sprayers, and sidewalks. It was the beginning of overstressed dinner parties, plumbing disasters, and a six-month period when Gilbert's little brother lived in the guest bedroom as he searched for a job.

Years later Anne would stand on her patio—the sound of traffic rushing in the distance, the stars obscured by smog—and raise her fist, shouting, "Who stole my Green Gables?"

I've spent the lion's share of my mental energy and physical effort working toward an ultimate life goal: domestic contentment. And I think I have found it, despite what my husband Matt might argue. Sure, he'll snicker and tell of my weekly tirades where I work all day, come home to read a decorating magazine, and then kick our sofa muttering, "Why can't you be more like your cousins at Pottery Barn?" But I digress.

Like all women, I have a secret and overwhelming urge to be a genetically spliced version of Martha Stewart and Ina Garten, with a dash of Sandra Lee thrown in for fun. I really like her hair.

Despite going to college and subsequently holding down a job, I spent years berating myself for my domestic limitations and disasters. I was shamed by my undersize area rugs, burned kitchen countertops, and a dog that insisted on pooping in the hallway during thunderstorms. But long before Martha, Ina, and Sandra combined in a big cloud of insecurity above my head, there was literature.

Most of us bookworms begin deluding ourselves from a young age. From the brooding mansions of Jane Eyre to the March sisters' New England farmhouse, we buried ourselves in the paper promises of fanciful homes, totally unprepared for the much less romantic reality we would one day face as grown-ups.

As gangly twelve-year-olds lying in the backyard, we constructed our dream homes from fiction. I personally saw myself (with magically transformed auburn hair just like a grown-up Anne Shirley) living on forty acres with my very own white farmhouse with curtains fluttering over apple pies cooling in the window. I called it Liz Gables. I don't know, don't ask.

There were several areas of miscalculation with this dream.

> 1. I'm a brunette. During my sophomore year in college I dyed my hair red to begin my Anne Shirley metamorphosis. I ended up looking like a jaundiced Ronald McDonald.

> 2. Our current home is smack dab in the middle of a sixty-year-old suburb full of oak trees and ranch homes in such close proximity that I could use the bathroom and simultaneously spit out the window on my neighbor's house.

3. If there are apple pies in our house, they come from Kroger and get reheated in the microwave. Some women fall into the category of phenomenal cooks, and then there are women like me who fall in the "Typhoid Mary" cooking category.

And so, after spending years imagining dwellings like Mr. Darcy's mansion or Nancy Drew's 1940s two-story colonial, we grow up and buy our first homes. We turn the brand-new doorknob, walk into an open floor plan with beige carpet and no crown molding, throw up our hands and say, "Who stole my spiral staircase? Where's the butler's pantry? Wait, what *is* a butler's pantry?"

I found myself comparing our home's square footage with that of Mr. Darcy's vast grounds. When I overcooked a pot roast, I wiped away a small tear and thought of Auntie Em's home-cooked farm food. When I couldn't afford an expensive sofa from Anthropologie, I found myself wishing for an estate sale at Wuthering Heights.

And then I stumbled upon a coping mechanism. When things went awry and off course in my own domestic universe, I projected reality onto my favorite literary friends. I pretended that Rhett Butler nicked his leg because he tried to trim weeds on the grounds of Tara while wearing a pair of shorts. I imagined Nancy Drew at her in-laws' house, surrounded by hick relatives who referred to squirrels as the "steak of the forest." I envisioned a cockroach crawling across the floor of the Capulets' dinner party.

All of my literary friends were plucked from their peaceful pages and tortured.

And as I proceeded to put these poor literary figures through the gristmill of reality, I realized there was much more to their stories than idyllic islands, lush fields, and sweeping manors. There was, at the center, the cog of friendship. Jo and Laurie, Elizabeth and Jane, Nancy and Bess, Anne and Diana; their stories leave us with reminders about what really matters. They cared for each other. They laughed with each other. They cried with each other. And when the chips were down, they rescued each other.

I don't know about you, but I love a good rescue. My favorite movie moments are the salvation moments. A woman is fighting off an intruder and—*bam!* Her neighbor kicks in the door and comes to her rescue. A family's car goes off the bridge and into a river and—*bam!* A Coast Guard boat fishes them out of the water. A rock climber loses his footing and clings helplessly to a mountain, and—*bam!* A rescue chopper lowers a ladder to safety. These deliverers appear just in the nick of time. They appear in planned ways that are not merely coincidental, but ordained by fate.

Heroic rescues are not the sole property of Hollywood. You find them in literature when Anne Shirley reenacts "The Lady of Shalott," nearly drowns, and Gilbert saves her. Scarlett shoots a Yankee soldier, and Melanie helps her hide the body. Marianne Dashwood twists her ankle, and Willoughby runs to her aid. Amy March falls through the pond just as Jo and Laurie turn back to skate to her rescue.

I love these moments, not just because they are romantic or action packed; I love what they represent. Beneath the pistol protection, dire emergencies, and perilous mountain climbs lies something more meaningful. It's a juxtaposition of perfectly timed redemption. Where something awful and ominous could have been, something positive thunders through the gloom and catastrophe. The sun rises. The chorus swells. These rescue scenes serve as reminders that perhaps a great plan is unfolding, that perhaps amid all the chaos and stranded souls in the world, destiny happens at critical moments.

This moment, for me, was defined by my friendship with a woman named Angela. And if I was meant to play the frenzied, temperamental Anne role, Angela most assuredly filled the loyal, levelheaded Diana shoes.

And like the Coast Guard ship or the rescue helicopter—Angela's friendship came to me during a dissatisfied, pivotal moment in which I needed her (but didn't know it yet). But there was another side of the coin. She needed me as well. She had a hard journey to face and needed a friend to walk it with her.

Our friendship wasn't an accident. It wasn't a coincidence. It was fate, with perhaps the slightest hint of salvation.

Chapter 1

Home Sweet Wuthering Home

The winds are sweeping across the moors and a large fireplace is crackling cozily at the end of an elegant sitting room. Rain peppers arched windows in lacy patterns as Heathcliff and Catherine enjoy hot tea under the protective roof of Wuthering Heights. And then, the peace is broken....

"Heathy, did you leave the water running in the kitchen?"

"No, why?"

"Hmmm . . . that's funny. I hear running water. You don't hear that? That trickle?"

Heathcliff shook his head, "Nah, I don't hear anything."

"With all due respect Heathy, I hear like a bat, and you have the decibel capacity of a water buffalo."

Heathcliff's eyes narrowed, "Why of all the names in the world that you could choose from did you pick water buffalo? Is that what Edgar calls me when I'm not around?! It is, isn't it!?"

"Oh, shush!" *Catherine stood and her knitting fell to the floor.* "The sound is coming from the fireplace. Come look at this."

Heathcliff rose, running a hand through his rakish hair as he stood next to Catherine, gazing up at the ancient stone fireplace. There, before them, flowed a small river. It ran from the top of the ceiling, ambled between the rocks and grout, spilled over the mantle, and splattered onto the hearth.

"I thought you said the roofers fixed the flashing on that leak?" Catherine said, hands on her hips.

Heathcliff's forehead wrinkled into a thousand angry crevices as he pounded his fist into his hand. "So help me, when I get hold of those roofers, I'll kick the living crap out of them."

"Now Heathy, calm down." Catherine gingerly patted his back. "Remember your temper. Let's practice those breathing techniques we talked about. Breathe, one, two, three . . ."

"Calm down?! We paid those guys $5,700 to reroof the place! Not only did they pee in the backyard during their lunch breaks, but now we have Niagara Falls in the living room!"

Catherine watched her beloved rant and rave as he reached for his cell phone, ready for battle. She gave a deep sigh, grabbed a nearby quilt, and began mopping up the water trickling toward the rug. It was going to be a very, very long night.

Is it possible to predict who our dearest friends will be? Can we make a list of qualities and say, "Any best friend of mine will be outgoing and preferably drive a low emission car because, you know, the environment is very important to me"?

I think we all know the answer. Friendships are no different than true love. They can't be planned or predicted; they come into our lives like great gusts of wind that knock things off the shelves and force us to stretch ourselves in uncomfortable yet beautiful ways. Sometimes friendship strikes like lightning and you know, instantly, that you and that person will be friends when you're old. You know that the two of you will be grumpy little old ladies shopping in Kohl's, arguing with the staff about sale prices and the proximity of the nearest parking space.

It was that way when I met Angela.

Of course, at the time, a cosmically ordained friendship was the furthest thing from my mind. The only thing I could focus on was my new home. Just one month earlier, my husband Matt and I had joined the leagues of new homeowners, oblivious to the housing bubble about to burst. I, however, approached this financial commitment with my default reaction: pessimism. It's in my DNA.

When I was a child, my parents gave me a fantastic dollhouse for Christmas. Instead of reveling in the bright green bathroom with shower, or the sleek minivan, or the spiral staircase in the living room, I leaned down, examined the plastic foundation, and said, "I think this place has termite damage."

When I was eight I cried for an entire afternoon because I'd left my bike outside during a snowstorm. "Rust damage is irreversible," I wailed.

At age twelve I informed mom, "If we don't do something about the mold growing on the ceiling over the shower, we'll all develop serious lung problems."

At age sixteen I passed on buying a car and bummed rides from friends instead stating, "Are you kidding? The blue book value on one of those tin cans plummets the moment you drive it off the lot."

Now in my twenties, I sat at the front desk of an office, stewing like a pot full of bubbling tomatoes, worrying that our new house was besieged by invisible fungus or pipes that contained lead.

Having graduated a few years earlier with an English degree, my ego had taken a beating. Actually, my ego had been escorted to a giant courtyard, chained to a pole, and publically flogged. You see, all English majors have lofty goals. We picture ourselves as great authors with castles in Scotland or beach homes in Key West where we'll pen great works of literature. We imagine ourselves at book signings wearing swoopy shawls with writerly glasses.

The reality is, if an English major lands a job answering phones and has health insurance, she's already ahead of the pack. And while I might not have succeeded in very many things in life, I was determined to be the very best home-owner in the universe. I planned to funnel every ounce of energy into perfecting my own Green Gables, my own mini kingdom of folded laundry and sparkling toilet bowls.

So there I was answering phones and wearing a swoopy shawl and writerly glasses in case anyone wanted me to autograph a purchase order. We were interviewing candidates for another position in the office, and Angela arrived first. She walked brusquely through the doors wearing a suit, her long dark hair pinned into a bun.

"I'm here for the interview. I'm Angela."

She was businesslike, but not unfriendly.

"Nice to meet you."

I reached out to shake her hand just as my boss, Darren, barked from his office, "Elizabeth, have you checked to see if there's legal paper in the copy room? I hope you didn't forget to order it."

I took a deep sigh and closed my eyes, fighting to extinguish the flames that had erupted at my feet and swooshed over the top of my head. Of course I'd remembered. He'd mentioned it thirty-six times in forty-eight hours, shouting from his desk like a passive-aggressive turtle yelling from the safety of his shell. I took another deep, cleansing breath. It didn't work. I'd read Tolstoy, and this jerk was nagging me about legal paper. When I opened my eyes, Angela was watching me in silence, an amused crinkle at the corners of her bright green eyes.

She smiled graciously and seated herself in the waiting area across from my desk. She was only a few years older than me, yet her appearance was impeccable, as if she'd stepped out of a more civilized era. She didn't slump. Her nails were trimmed in perfect crescents. Art-Deco era earrings bobbed above her shoulders. Peeping out of her bag was a copy of *The Importance of Being Earnest*.

I was sure, after having only known her for thirty seconds, that she was a paragon of good manners, well-read, self-assured, quiet, and loyal. She was also, no doubt, quirky. After all, how many people bring along an Oscar Wilde book to an interview?

She caught me staring and smiled politely. But behind the smile lay a certain determination that sprung from what my grandmother describes as "grit." The smile said in no uncertain terms, "It's lovely to meet you, dear stranger, but it's terribly rude to stare."

I smiled back and leaned forward. "Sorry, we don't get many visitors during the day. I didn't mean to inspect you."

She smiled, this time warmly. "That's perfectly all right. I completely understand. I worked in an isolated office at my last job. I spent every day filing papers, returning phone calls, dusting my keyboard, and exploring the Internet for information on English castles and scone recipes. I got excited when the coffee salesman came to take our order. When I got home I'd ask my husband to take my pulse, just to make sure I was still alive and not in some sort of administrative purgatory."

I laughed and pointed to the book hanging from her bag, "I see you like Oscar Wilde."

"No, I *love* Oscar Wilde. I see you like to read as well?" she asked, examining the stack of books on my desk.

I nodded. "I actually majored in English."

Most people found this bit of information surprising. After all, the general public usually places the receptionist in the same hierarchical category with waitresses and janitors. Telling them you have a college degree usually throws an uncomfortable vibe into the air, an imbalance to the American class system. But I believe you can tell everything you need to know about a person's character by observing how much they tip or if they greet the custodian mopping the lobby.

Angela didn't bat an eye. "I'm working on my master's in English. Please tell me you hate Faulkner."

I bugged my eyes and nodded excitedly. Hating Faulkner is something no self-respecting Southerner is supposed to admit. I liked her instantly.

At that moment Darren waddled from his doorway. He was a short man, endowed with a beefy figure and an uncomfortable ability to arrange entire conversations around his previous profession as a farmer. This sort of strange segue was really just his creepy way of discussing uncomfortable, inappropriate things with female coworkers—in other words, with me. In short, he was odd and pervy.

One minute he would expound the merits of a proper filing system and out of nowhere he'd shift into farm-pervert mode. "But how does the baby cow know to find the nipple? I mean, it's a miracle, the fact that he knows to find the nipple. I think it's evidence of God's beautiful plan, that babies know how to find the nipple." Of course, I believed our conversations had nothing to do with God's plan, but merely his sicko inclination to discuss nipples with a secretary thirty years his junior.

Angela had no way of knowing this as she followed him into the interview. I wanted to warn her, to flag her down and say, "Watch out! He's a pervert." But as she passed by my desk, she gazed down on my well-worn copy of *Anne of Green Gables* and smiled widely, giving me a wink as she whispered almost inaudibly, "He looks like Boss Hogg, but I think we should call him 'Toad.'"

I watched her vanish behind closed doors and knew immediately that she, like Anne's Diana, would be my friend, a true kindred spirit. After all, we had already forged our own secret code word in a matter of minutes. Toad, indeed. It would be only a matter of weeks before I got a job in another department and leaped out from underneath Toad's thumb. But despite my knowledge that I would soon be in another office down the hall, I hoped they would hire her. I sincerely longed for a friend at work. I dreamed of having someone to commiserate with, to go to lunch with, and to suffer alongside when Darren went on tangents or made inappropriate comments.

After Angela's interview was over she gave me a friendly wave and I shot her a thumbs up sign. As hopeful as I was that she would be hired, I didn't have much time to think about it. Matt and I were meeting after work to begin painting our new house, and I could see gloomy gray clouds on the horizon.

Despite a clean bill of health from our inspector, I just knew there was something horribly wrong lurking beneath those cheerful 1950s ranch walls. I was also suffering from my "ladies' time" which frankly, renders me incapable of cheerful behavior. PMS combined with the adult burden of great debt swirled above my head, creating a toxic cocktail of negative emotions.

Basically, I was on a tear.

And while I'm a dyed in the wool, yellow dog pessimist, I married a good-hearted optimist. To sufficiently describe Matt, I'll quote my greatest hero, Erma Bombeck: *"Most of us can't be like the optimist who was given a barn full of fertilizer and ran through it pell mell shouting, 'I know there's a pony here somewhere.'"*

Matt comes home from work, takes off his shoes, sighs, and says, "Gosh it's good to be home."

I come home from work, kick my shoes across the room, and shriek about the traffic.

Matt opens the mailbox with eager anticipation of finding a fun magazine or a coupon for steaks.

I open the mailbox and stare into its depths, expecting nothing but bills and bad news.

As Erma pointed out, Matt enters the barn looking for a pony, and I sniff the air and say, "It smells like crap in here."

It was getting dark as we pulled into the carport, unloaded the vats of wall paint we'd just purchased, and unlocked the door. It was our goal to complete all the painting before we moved in the furniture—a wise yet ambitious plan for two newbie homeowners. Frankly, I'd never even wielded a paint-brush before.

Matt fiddled with the keys a second-and-a-half too long and I clutched my throat, blurting, "We're going to have to get that door handle changed, I bet it's broken!"

"It's not broken," Matt stated, opening the door easily and ushering me inside.

Instead of reveling in our first home, instead of skipping like Julie Andrews and spinning with outspread skirts in our empty formal living room, I glared acidly at the lavender-and-lime-green walls (courtesy of the previous fun-house-color-loving owners).

"These original colors are brighter than I remember, we should have bought primer. Regular paint will never cover this."

"It will be fine," Matt said as he began opening the lid to the first paint can.

"Don't spill it!" I yelped, eyeing the floor. "Hey, do you remember this big scratch in the hardwood when we were here last time?"

Matt paused, staring upward in silent prayer, perhaps not that God might turn me into a pillar of salt, but just render me temporarily mute.

"Liz, you're going to have to calm down."

As I glared unflinchingly into my husband's eyes, I knew he was right. I knew I should calm down, unclench, and reboot. But I also knew there was no way that was going to happen.

"Well, all I'm saying is . . . that's a huge scratch. It looks like Lizzie Borden dragged a hatchet across the floor. And look at that crooked light fixture! I don't remember it being that hideous. Do you think that's damaged the wiring? I'm calling our agent."

What happened next is a bit blurry. Matt called me a Negative Nellie. I accused him of being an ostrich or a big buffoon, I can't really remember which. But what I do remember was being mid-yell during the sentence, "I'm *not* negative, I'm just realistic!" when I realized that every window in the house was standing wide open.

My eyes bulged. I pointed wordlessly to the front window as a dove began to coo outside. "Now look what you've done!"

"*What?*" Matt shot back.

"The neighbors are going to think we're crazy!" I stamped my foot.

"The neighbors won't think *I'm* crazy," Matt said, returning to his paint can.

And at that moment the doorbell rang.

A normal person would have noticed the lovely couple from next door standing on the front porch with a plate full of welcome cookies. A normal person would have hidden her head in shame at the open windows and the new acquaintances that were sure to have heard us call each other "Nitwit" and "Scab Picker." But instead I cocked my head and listened with zealous glee to the warbled, off-key, dying-bird sound that was our doorbell with the triumph of a gladiator who had just speared his opponent through the jugular.

"*Seeeee!*" I hissed loudly at Matt. "I *told* you something was wrong with this house. Just listen to that cacophony the sellers called a doorbell!"

"*Shhhhhh* . . ." Matt gently pushed me aside. "Try not to scare them."

Our new neighbors, Mason and Deanna, turned out to be lovely people. Matt and I chatted and smiled, faking marital bliss like two seasoned con artists. At one point I think we even held hands, despite the fact that only minutes before I had threatened to rip off a piece of drywall to prove there was black mold growing just out of sight.

After they said goodbye, leaving us with a plate of delicious chocolate chip cookies, I began to feel remorse. Or it could have been the fact that the magical properties in the chocolate were soothing the monstrous PMS beast lurking behind my seemingly placid exterior.

"I'm sorry," I said, chomping the cookies. "I don't know what's come over me."

Matt patted my shoulder. "That's okay."

I swallowed another cookie whole. "Let's just start painting. I'll feel better."

And so we did. We spread out the plastic, turned on the radio, and spent the next two hours turning the walls in our bright lavender living room to bridal gown white. It was fun. It was blissful. It was stress free. I breathed a sigh of relief as the tension slowly left my chest; the stress headache in the back of my head began to lessen. There were no broken windows or uneven floors. There was no need to replace the heat and air unit, the doors were secure. Our kitchen cabinets were old but clean, and there wasn't a single problem that couldn't be solved with a little bit of paint and a new light fixture.

All was right with the world. We washed our paintbrushes out in the kitchen sink, cleaned up, and exited through the garage door.

"That was fun," I said.

"Do you feel better now?" Matt smiled.

I took a deep breath. "Absolutely."

"Good," Matt kissed the top of my head and unlocked my car door.

And then I looked down.

Below my feet, flowing peacefully like the Nile, was a wide, babbling stream of white water. It flowed merrily like a brook across the carport, under the car, and down the driveway.

My voice became very low and I blinked a few times, recognizing that this could very well be the catastrophe that finally gave me a massive heart attack at the ripe old age of twenty-six.

"Matt, what is that?"

Matt's face was pale in the moonlight, horror written all over his normally peaceful features. "I think we have a leaky pipe."

I inhaled the clean night air through both my nostrils as hard and fast as I could, doing everything possible to stay on my feet and not scream like a baby at a bris.

And then, the unthinkable happened. Matt got really, really angry.

"Dangit!" He threw his keys to the ground."It's all the water from the sink in the kitchen running out from under the house! That's why it's white! It's paint water! The water we just used to clean the brushes!"

It was a life-changing occurrence. When faced with an angry Matt—something that happened only about as often as a full eclipse—I found myself feeling the urge to do something I had never done before in my entire life: stay calm.

"Okay, let's just think about this." I tested out my non-screaming voice much like a child trying out a bicycle for the first time.

"*No!*" Matt was roaring now. "That inspector promised us that the pipes looked great. And look at this! It's the biggest leak I've ever seen!"

Here stood a man who had taken every last dime he'd ever earned, and a hefty donation from his parents, and sunk it into the American Dream: his first home. And right now, that leaky-piped home was metaphorically peeing all over him.

"Is this going to stain the concrete?" I asked quietly.

"*Probably!*" He kicked a paint can out of the way and reached for the hose, turning on the water. "I'm going to try to wash it off before it has time to dry."

There we stood, in the moonlight, washing white paint water from the foundation of the house, through the carport, and all the way down the driveway. It was at this point, like so many other times in my life, that I thought to myself, "This can't get much worse."

And then it did.

An elderly couple ambled down the street, hand in hand, walking their dachshund in the evening moonlight. I saw them approaching, but Matt was deep in concentration as he held the water hose at full blast, trying to keep his driveway free of the whitewash water. I gave them a half wave, hoping they'd pass by without incident. No such luck.

"Hey there, son . . ." the old gentleman waved genially, "I think you're a little mixed up watering that concrete. You're supposed to turn that hose on the grass, unless you like helping the weeds in the cracks of the driveway."

His blue-haired wife chuckled, evidently finding her jokester husband very clever.

Matt's head jerked upright, his eyes filled with rage as I tried to motion the couple to run as fast as their little pacemakers and artificial hips would allow.

"Of course I'm not watering the weeds!" Matt bellowed, "I've got paint running down the driveway of my house! What does it look like I'm doing?"

I shrugged apologetically, wondering when Matt and I had suddenly switched personalities. In a normal, orderly world I was the "kerosene and matches" half of the relationship. I roared with outrage when the postman accidentally delivered our neighbor's mail to our porch. I flipped out when the checkbook didn't balance to the exact cent. But Matt was the other half, the calm half. He only got upset when fast food drive-through workers accidentally put raw onions on his cheeseburger. But on that night, it appeared that we had swapped places.

The elderly couple whispered something about "crazy youngsters and their drugs" and continued down the road.

I turned to Matt. "Let's just go get some rest."

Matt slumped and sat on the driveway. "I know. I'm sorry I got so mad."

I knelt next to him. "That's okay, honey. I understand. But do you remember what I was talking about earlier?"

Matt nodded. "Yes, next time I find myself in a happy situation I'll just do what you do."

"Which is?"

"Expect the worst," he sighed. "You were right. There was something wrong with the house."

I nodded as we got up and trudged toward the car. "Come on, we'll go get a cheeseburger."

We left our new house behind, the remnants of white paint on our driveway. I learned that sometimes, it's up to me to be positive and look on the bright side. And Matt learned that every now and then, life's barn does not contain a pony.

CHAPTER 2

Gone with Your Sanity: Paint Colors

"Rhett!"

"What?" Rhett rounded the corner of the house.

Scarlett squinted critically at his disheveled appearance. "What's wrong with you?"

"Dadgum weed eater cut my leg again," he sniffled, hunching over to examine his lacerated calf muscle.

Scarlett eyed her husband, hunkered and moaning softly over three barely perceptible cuts. She sighed. "And why do you think that happened?"

"Because I was wearing my cargo shorts again," he mumbled, not making eye contact.

"Ugh, I've told you a billion times to wear long pants." She rolled her eyes. "Can you concentrate for just one minute? I need your opinion."

Rhett grimaced. "But don't you think you should put some hydrogen peroxide on this or something? Do you know where the Band-aids are? I don't want to get infected . . ."

"Oh, for crying out loud. They're tiny cuts. Now focus please! Look at these paint colors and tell me which one you like best for the new siding."

Rhett glared at his insensitive wife. He'd long suspected she didn't care whether he lived or died, and now he knew she cared more about paint colors than she did his soon-to-be-gangrenous leg.

Rhett puffed out his chest and crossed his arms, eyeing the three color shades she'd painted on the side of the house. A familiar feeling of obstinacy rose up in his chest.

"Well, I hate number one. It looks like that awful pea soup you made last week."

Scarlett's jaw locked and an almost imperceptible puff of steam rose from the top of her head.

"Number two looks like axle grease. Hate that."

He stole a sideways glance in time to see Scarlett silently mouthing profanities.

"And number three, well, that's the same shade of red that Belle Watling painted her new business establishment. I guess I prefer that one."

"You're such a jerk!" Scarlett roared, throwing her paintbrush at Rhett, who expertly ducked the projectile. Shrugging, he turned to leave. After all, he had hydrogen peroxide to find and gangrene to stop.

"Don't you even care what color we paint the house?" She was still shrieking, unconcerned as up and down the street the lace curtains ruffled and neighbors looked on.

"Frankly, my dear," Rhett didn't turn back, "I don't give a crap."

Choosing the right wall color carries with it the weight of life's biggest decisions. Somehow, our society has elevated this selection process (on level of importance) straight to the top of the chart. It hovers somewhere between choosing a spouse and what kind of haircut defines your personality.

Each shade of the rainbow evokes a certain emotion, reveals a specific character quirk. They truly have a life of their own. Where's my proof? The Department of Homeland Security's terror alert system. If their highest alert level—"severe"—were represented by pale pink, I doubt we'd take it seriously. We'd draw deep breaths and think of cotton candy and Ferris wheels, ignoring the suspicious package left lying unattended as we searched for roasted peanuts and fresh-squeezed lemonade. Instead, the savvy folks at Homeland Security chose the color red, which makes me simultaneously hungry and nervous as I glance at the sky to make sure King Kong isn't lumbering into my suburban neighborhood.

Some people are adventurous with color. I suspect they're the very same people who as kindergartners fought for crayons during art time, yelling, "Magenta is my favorite color. Give it!"

I admire people like that. I am not one of them. I was the kindergartner slouching in the corner, wiping my runny nose, and obligingly coloring with the leftover shades of Sienna Dirt and Gray Blah.

I'll spray-paint a baroque-framed mirror turquoise in a heartbeat, but when it comes to the vast surfaces of walls, my throat closes up and I search for an EpiPen. I fear being surrounded in a smothering shade of brown or a hyper yellow hue. I worry about waking up and shrieking in horror at neon green walls and yelling, "Who let Slimer in here?" I treat the process of choosing a paint color the very same way I treat loved ones when they have the flu: with dread and avoidance.

I never realized the depth of this color phobia until after we painted almost every room in our house white. I was ashamed. Every visitor and relative said the same thing.

"You picked white, huh? Well, I guess it's good to play it safe sometimes. Look on the bright side, white walls make the rooms look bigger."

I was gripped with panic. Apparently I'd made a mistake. Apparently (at least according to every TV show and decorating magazine in existence), white was a cowardly, boring choice. I set about to change it immediately.

I stood in the paint aisle at Lowe's and struggled to breathe as a salesperson named Lydia waited on me.

"Do you like warm colors? How about Adobe Blush?" Lydia smiled helpfully.

"I'm not sure, I can't really feel my hands right now," I said, my eye twitching inexplicably as I wiped the cold sweat from my brow.

"Or, if you prefer cooler tones, you could go with Olive Latte."

I eyed a paint chip that reminded me of baby spit-up and clutched a nearby end cap for support.

"Are you going to use one neutral color throughout the home, or do varying shades in each room? Flow is very important."

The room began to spin and I could feel the blood draining from my face.

"How about this," Lydia patted me on the shoulder. "I'll mix up several cans of paint samples and you can take them home and test them on your walls. That way, you'll have a way to try them out without committing."

"Okay," I said pathetically as she led me to the paint counter like a mother leading a child into the doctor's office for a shot.

Off I trudged, laden with dozens of tiny paint cans. I practiced deep breathing as I headed for home, headed for Matt's help and soothing advice. I was not to find it.

Matt immediately got a look on his face that read pure panic. He warily surveyed my 142 cans of paint samples, knowing that the wrong opinion could get him into mountains of trouble.

"Just paint little swatches on one wall, and then I'll help you pick."

I glared as he retreated like a coward into the den. And so I began, alone, trying out sample after sample, painting neat orderly squares on the wall. It soon became apparent that decoding paint color names is as complicated as balancing a checkbook or trying to clean a toilet without actually touching its ceramic surface. The lovely, lilting descriptors assigned to each color were soothing and poetic, but the reality was another story entirely.

Spring Fog
What you think it's like: A lovely grayish green color, the color of budding trees partially hidden behind a drifting wall of London fog.
What it actually looks like: What your dog threw up after he ate a bunch of grass and a stray slug from the patio wall.

Russet Sunset
What you think it's like: The subtle reds in a desert sunset, the warmth shining on your face as you stand before an endless horizon of blazing loveliness.
What it actually looks like: It's just plain red. Bright red. And to make matters worse, it actually looks pink for the first five coats. On the eighth coat you put on sunglasses, stare at the walls and say, "I've made a big mistake."

Hyacinth Stroll
What you think it's like: A chilly spring day. You walk down a peaceful woodland path, calming lilac-hued hyacinths popping up out of the wet ground. You deeply inhale their scent and are at utter peace with the world around you.
What it actually looks like: Barney. It looks like a giant, purple dinosaur. Which would be fine if your dining room were a daycare. But it's not.

Goldenrod Afternoon

What you think it's like: A sunny afternoon, the air filled with bright rays of cheerfulness as you soak up the vitamin D.

What it actually looks like: A blinding shade of yellow gold coins, reminiscent of the decor at Caesars Palace. You don't appreciate it when your husband suggests adding a naked Roman statue to the corner of the living room.

Coastal Storm

What you think it's like: The swirling grayness of the sky as you stand on the New England coast, rocks and crashing waves down below you, the wind blowing your hair.

What it actually looks like: Black. Basically you've just painted your sitting room walls black. It looks like a cave and your teenage neighbor thinks it's "just the coolest."

And so I fought the urge to rotate my head and levitate above the floor as I gazed at my smorgasbord of color confusion. Instead, I plated two Hostess cupcakes and gave up, choosing instead to watch people on TV make progress on their beautifully designed and remodeled homes as I stole sideways glances at my headache-inducing color swatches.

The days passed and our walls remained white. No color. No decisions. No peace.

In the meantime my new coworker and friend Angela did her best to distract me. Our friendship formed quickly within our first few days of working together. It felt like fate had taken us by the hands and said, "Liz, this is Angela. Angela, this is Liz. We think you'll be good for each other."

We spent our lunch breaks sitting on a park bench, reading together and comparing story ideas for novels we planned to write. We dreamed of one day seeing our books on the shelf of a bookstore.

"Just to hold a book in my hands, a book I wrote, is my greatest dream. Anything else that came of it would just be icing," Angela proclaimed, and I couldn't have agreed more.

We both had deep, loving, and at times tumultuous bonds with our younger sisters. She nicknamed her younger sister Anna "Zelda" as a tribute to F. Scott's spunky and rambunctious wife. I named one of my younger sisters Manuel Noriega because of her proclivity toward decapitating my Barbies and using their heads as weapons.

We also shared a similar, albeit different, verbal reaction to sexist men. This was probably Toad's fault—with all his talk of cow nipples and descriptions of his urine flow measurements at the doctor's office. Once, during a business lunch, we sat across the table from a man who stated, "I've never allowed my wife to wear shorts. Frankly, it's distasteful and immodest."

Both of our gazes carried the scorching condemnation of dragon's fire, but the way we verbalized it later was quite different. I said something along the lines of, "What a gigantic dork. If I had to live with a jerk like that, I'd kill him."

Angela, on the other hand, stated in ladylike clipped phonetics, "What an enormous old sober-sides. If I had to live with some prehistoric caveman like that, I'd asphyxiate him."

She'd spent her childhood in Arkansas and later moved to Florida, but her accent carried none of the harsh notes of hillbilly-dom, and she spoke only in crisply pronounced syllables. She collected books, painted in her free time, and quoted T.S. Eliot like the rest of us quote lines from *Everybody Loves Raymond*. Frankly, she could have easily been a turn-of-the-century graduate of Bryn Mawr who touted feminism and the benefits of a good bubble bath. Oftentimes when we were together I felt like a big-haired, overly loud Dolly Parton out to lunch with Katharine Hepburn. But somehow, our friendship worked. It was easy.

In every friendship there's what I like to think of as a "cement moment." It's a moment where two women realize they've crossed over the bridge from "occasional lunch date" friends to "I love you and would be willing to come over to your house and clean up after your dogs with a pooper-scooper" friends. It's a moment when friendship begins to resemble family rather than a Junior League luncheon.

That's what happened with Angela on the day I cut my hair off.

From afar, our coworkers had begun to comment that we looked like sisters. As far as facial characteristics went, we really didn't resemble each other. Angela had calm, cat-like eyes and an aristocratic nose. Her pale face was classic, stoic, and controlled. I had the tendency to splash every emotion right across my face like a billboard; when I was nervous, my hazel eyes blinked rapidly and my lips pursed into a thin line.

The real reason our coworkers commented on our similarities was, coincidentally, color related. We both had long hair in similar shades of brunette.

Angela had lovely, dark, Lady Godiva hair with natural curl and sheen. It flowed in flattering waves around her forehead and down her back. And even though she was showing a few early grays around her temples, they only seemed to add to her follicly blessed beauty. Her hair caused men to pause and stare (not that she ever noticed).

My hair, on the other hand, just looked like a constant mess. It was frizzy around the forehead, shoved into a haphazard, uneven bun at the base of my neck. Long hair was not a facet of beauty for me. It was just another example of my tendency to put off salon visits. For years.

So one day, while I continued to bemoan our house's lack of color character, I made what some would later declare a rash decision to cut and color my hair. This was going to be major. I might not have been able to find the perfect shade of mint green for my kitchen, but I had found a magazine picture with the exact shade of blonde highlights I wanted for my hair.

Angela told me to go for it. Actually what she said was something along the lines of, "By all means, do what you feel suits you."

And so I did. I took the morning off work and marched into a salon.

Two hours later the ground below me was covered in mounds of shorn locks. My head felt so much lighter, like it might float away. I looked in the mirror at my new chin-length, blonde-highlighted bob and took a deep breath.

"I bet you've lost a good five pounds!" The hairdresser was pleased with herself in that way all hairdressers are when they garner a new convert to the "constant maintenance" hair church.

I glanced sideways at her, disconcerted by her comment.

"Your hair." She pointed down at the brunette carpeting beneath our feet. "I bet that weighed five pounds. And those blonde highlights really brighten up your face."

Nevertheless, I worried. As I returned to work, the back of my neck uncharacteristically cool and bare, I fretted. For years I'd forgone changing my hair for fear that I would be inducted into the tiny-head big-bottom league. Perhaps this was because of my Southern heritage, where women believe heartily that hair should be long and big to balance out the rest of your body.

I walked into work brusquely. Raisin-head shelf-bottom or no, if I walked fast enough, people wouldn't be able to notice. And that's when I heard this phrase screeched from the end of the hallway: "Oh mah gawwwwd, Elizabeth. What did you do to yourself?"

Felicia, otherwise known to all employees as "Coffee Breath," was pointing and running toward me.

"Why would you do that? Why in the world would you cut all that pretty hair off?"

It felt like a bad movie. The hallway seemed to stretch out to a skinny tunnel as her voice gained in high-pitched volume.

Once, at a funeral, Felicia had walked up to the mourning family and stated loudly, "You know, black people just don't look the same when they die as white people. Whites turn colors." She was, in a word, ignorant, not to mention slightly racist.

"You know when them blonde streaks grow out your roots will look just awful. And I bet your husband's gonna be real mad. . . . You know the men-folk don't like women with short hair."

Now she was right up in my face, her tiny piercing eyes and rank caffeinated breath infringing on my personal space. I held my breath, praying that God wouldn't let me lose my job when I knocked her lights out.

That's when I heard Angela's voice cut through the air like a knife through curdled milk.

"Felicia, what in heaven's name is wrong with you?"

Felicia stopped mid-sentence, shocked into silence. Her blustering, slightly uneducated demeanor was something that most of us just avoided. She was not accustomed to being confronted.

Angela marched toward us. She looked like she was on the verge of morphing into a lightning bolt–wielding superhero. I forgot all about my short hair and Felicia's moldy coffee breath. Angela looked downright frightening.

"Elizabeth, I think your new hair is chic and modern," she reassured me before turning back to Felicia. "You are incredibly rude and need to learn the art of keeping your unfiltered thoughts to yourself."

Felicia's eyes were giant saucers. Amazed and indignant, she replied, "Angela, I don't have a problem with y'all, but I just speak my mind, and if you don't like it well then . . ."

"No, you are correct. I don't like it. No one does. I also don't like your lack of grammatical skill. I don't like your total absence of social awareness. And I truly dislike the fact that you wear sweatpants in lieu of slacks at least once a week. If you cannot muster a compliment for Elizabeth's lovely new haircut, then I suggest you go back to your office. *Silently.*"

I stood dumbfounded with my mouth agape. When I was ten, a neighbor boy punched me in the stomach over an argument about a bicycle. As I tumbled to the ground, I saw my sister Rebecca, age four, vault off the front porch, grab a nearby stick, and proceed to flail the boy's legs as he retreated from our yard. Never before or since had anyone defended me like that, until now.

Felicia stomped back down the hall mumbling a string of "Well I nevers."

Angela turned to me, her lips pursed, the color returning to her face.

"Don't take this the wrong way," I began carefully. "But you're scary when you're mad."

Angela smiled and straightened her red cardigan. "I'll take that as a compliment. Truthfully, I cannot abide that woman. Her manners are atrocious. And your hair really is very cute."

I realized then and there, as she glared icily at Felicia's retreating back, that even if Angela had hated my new hair, she would still be next to me with her hands on her hips.

I realized it was our cement moment. Angela was my true friend, a friend willing to do battle to protect me. I realized no amount of hair length, crass coworkers, or little-head big-bottom syndromes would ever change that.

I did end up loving my new haircut and color (despite my lingering fear that once the highlights grew out I would look like a skunk with a reverse stripe). I did not, however, come to terms with the fact that the walls in my house remained unpainted and plain.

Angela continued to listen to my paint color woes and grumbles with the same patience and sage wisdom that she used when I bemoaned Matt's refusal to use the dirty clothes hamper, or my dog's persistent, catlike foot licking. She was also a genius, using distraction as her greatest tool in our friendship.

And so she took my mind off my household troubles, sending me interesting websites about paintings of European royalty. We discussed their clothing, life histories, and beautiful gardens. We longed to be elegant women in sweeping dresses and thick braids, standing regally as an artist painted our portrait, lush English gardens behind us.

Our real-world portraits would have involved pantsuits, stacks of papers towering over our desks, and candy wrappers littering the floors of our offices.

Obviously, we preferred the whole royalty, garden thing.

Since it was early spring, we decided to create our own English gardens. We made a trip to the local nursery to peruse the rosebush roots. The owner assured us that roses very rarely bloom the same year after being planted. But as women who dreamed of regal yards, we were willing to be patient.

I fell instantly in love with a cheerful orange and pink rose called Fiesta. Of course, the only proof of its coloring was a picture on the tag (since the shrub was still in root form). Knowing Angela's affinity for all things related to royal families, I pointed across the aisle, "Look Ang, this one is called Queen Elizabeth."

Angela eyed the bright pink rose on the tag with distaste, "No thank you; I don't care for that color."

Angela preferred slightly sinister Victorian-style plants such as the Venus flytrap or any sort of teeth-baring plant cousin, which made sense to me after seeing her verbally fillet Felicia. She perused the next aisle and immediately began loading several small rose roots into her buggy.

I wrinkled my nose. "Those are black roses."

"They're not black, they're dark purple. The name is Cardinal de Richelieu. Isn't that fascinating?"

We carted the rose roots to our respective homes, planted them, and waited for our long-term investment in English garden living to blossom.

As spring grew bright green around us and I found myself gleefully wearing sandals again on the weekends, I tended my baby rose bushes. To my surprise and delight, one fragrant bud began to bloom.

I called Angela immediately. "Hey! You will never believe this, I have a bud blooming! I thought that wouldn't happen until next year. It's a gorgeous shade of coral."

"I have a rosebud as well." Angela's voice carried an air of brooding dissatisfaction.

"That's great!" I chirped, envisioning our future yards with great swaths of roses and trimmed hedges.

"Not really. Just come over and see," she said and hung up the phone.

Angela's house was a white split level with black shutters. Lush ferns hung from the porch and a large aloe plant rested by the front door. It was crisp and clean, with a no-nonsense air, just like her. When I arrived she was waiting outside, her gardening gloves and hat carefully in place. I was wearing cutoffs and flip-flops from the seventh grade.

Ignoring my sad attire she grabbed my hand. "Just look."

We rounded the corner of her house to examine the small rosebushes. They were sporting not one, but two rosebuds, each in a vivid shade of pink.

"Oh no!" I gasped.

Angela nodded solemnly, "It's that blasted Queen Elizabeth."

I bit my lip. "Can you live with the color pink?"

Angela's dark glare assured me she could not.

I knelt beside the small plants. "I guess the roots were mislabeled."

"I'd say so." She crossed her arms in disapproval of the girly hued flowers.

"Ang . . ." I sniffed the air. "What's that smell?"

"Gasoline," she answered pertly, motioning toward a small gas can at the edge of the house.

I sniffed the plants again. "Are you . . . pouring this on them?"

"Yes," Angela stated, her pale face shadowed beneath her hat, an expression of sheer determination written across her delicate features.

I sat on the ground, astounded. "You're killing your mislabeled roses?"

"*Pink* roses," Angela interjected.

"So you're poisoning them?" I tried to stifle a flood of giggles.

"The advertised pictures with these rose roots were blatant misrepresentations!" she insisted.

"Why don't we just dig them up and return them to the nursery instead?" I offered.

"No," Angela shook her head. "It's a matter of retribution."

I gazed at my ladylike friend's gardening attire, the assassin gas can on the lawn, and the rosebushes that were officially "walking the mile," and fell out in fits of laughter.

On the same fateful day that Angela sentenced her Queen Elizabeth plants to the guillotine, I drove promptly to Lowe's, purchased a gallon of paint, and began painting over my wall swatches.

"Wait, what's happening?" Matt asked, examining my color choice with confusion.

"I'm leaving the wall color exactly like it is." I stated, rolling a wide swath of original white paint over the painted squares.

"Why?" He'd never known me to give up on, well, anything in my entire life. He often referred to me lovingly as his little snapping turtle based on my inability to let go of anything. Ever.

"Because of Angela's roses."

Matt slumped into a nearby chair. "I'm seriously confused."

"The room is fine the way it is. It's bright, it's cheerful, and with white walls I can change my accessories whenever I want to."

Matt stared at me in disbelief, then exited the room in a fog of total bewilderment, choosing to say no more on the topic. He's supersmart that way.

You see, I realized that perfection, especially when it involves color, is next to impossible. My paint samples weren't even close to the color perfection I had imagined in my mind's eye, just like Angela's faux Cardinal de Richelieu roses were imperfect Queen Elizabeth impostors intent on foiling her garden plans. Even my lovely blonde highlights were growing out quickly, leaving behind dark roots.

There's nothing wrong with painting a room, of course, but in watching Angela's pink rose debacle, and examining my own battle against misleading paint color names, I realized maybe status quo wasn't such a bad thing after all. And so I chose to leave the living room white. Instead of covering the walls in color, I bought red pillows and spray painted a mirror frame turquoise. I chose to stop gnawing my fingernails over the colors of the rainbow and instead to appreciate the fact that there are colors of the rainbow.

Angela's roses? Miraculously they survived the gasoline gauntlet and are still alive and well. And while there may not be such a thing as color perfection, there are perfect friendships. And unlike wilting flowers or trendy paint colors, some friendships grow roots in your heart where they live and thrive forever.

Chapter 3

Pay No Attention to the Dog Behind the Curtain

If Dorothy had heard it once, she'd heard it a bazillion times.

"I don't know how you live with all those tornadoes. I just couldn't do it."

Floods and tornadoes are, sadly enough, as common in her neck of the woods as late garbage service, long lines at the carwash, and misdelivered mail are in the suburbs. When the nationally syndicated news networks show up with camera crews to film scenes of carnage and destruction, they are usually met by men wearing camo with chain saws strapped to their backs. Sometimes they're met with scenes of local Hells Angels setting up hot-dog grilling in the parking lot of the Piggly Wiggly to feed the poor and misplaced victims.

Sometimes, if they're lucky, the news crews are met by Dorothy's cousin, a gap-toothed man named Silas, eyes ablaze with excitement as he points his crooked pinky finger (the result of a snipe-hunting accident in his youth) to the mountains and yells into the microphone, "That tornado jumped over that there horizon just like a spinny top I got one time for Christmas when

I was just a little thing and my great-granny pulled it out of a Cracker Jack box and wrapped it for me shore as shootin'."

But Dorothy had a slightly different outlook. She had, unlike the rest of them, been sucked up into a twister's vortex. She had hung out with witches and a brainless scarecrow (who was not to be confused with the witless wonder she'd just broken up with). And for the past ten years she had possessed the uncanny ability to predict tornadoes.

That was exactly what was happening now. The hairs on the back of Dorothy's neck sprung to attention and a familiar twitchy feeling took root in the pit of her stomach. She accepted the fact that she was Kansas's human barometer. People might not have believed that she went to Oz or tripped the light fantastic in a field of poppies, but when Dorothy started running during a storm, the townsfolk did likewise.

The winds kicked up as she gripped her umbrella and exited the general store where she worked. The sky above was the palest shade of green, the clouds shifting like the ADD students in her Sunday Bible class.

She had to get home to Toto.

The winds gusted stronger as she ran down the side road that led to her little farmhouse. It was just a small two-bedroom home with white siding and roses climbing up the front trellis. She loved it—it was her home. But right now, she was most concerned for Toto. She reached down, removed the flip-flops that impeded her stride, and proceeded to sprint, running barefoot down the dirt road as the wind blew harder.

Toto was her best friend. When she gazed deep within his brown eyes, Dorothy always knew he believed her. He too had come back from Oz a changed dog. For instance, Toto had taken such a liking to the munchkins and their friendly dog-loving ways (not to mention special liverwurst treats) that he now hated all tall people. He also hated storms. In fact, Dorothy usually found Toto crammed beneath the front parlor couch (which was a feat in and of itself since he had gained the human equivalent of one hundred pounds over the last ten years).

Toto understood when no one believed her about the Wicked Witch or the Emerald City. He crawled in bed with her every night, his big eyes blinking, his ever-widening behind wagging in support.

She ran faster.

The sky grew black and claps of thunder rattled the walls. She unlatched the front door, threw her purse and shoes onto the floor, and flipped on the television just in time to see beeping alerts scrolling across the bottom of the screen. And then the lights went out as the tornado sirens began to wail.

"Toto!" She ran to the sofa, knelt down, and peered into the dark shadows underneath.

A pair of wide eyes greeted her. Dorothy grabbed Toto's front legs, dragging him like an angry, wet cat from his too-small hiding place.

She jumped to her feet and rushed down the long hallway that ran the length of the house toward the back door. As she raced barefoot across the wooden floors, she slipped on something slick. She flew through the darkness, shrieking, trying to keep herself upright and hold onto Toto as he trembled in her arms, the sirens wailing louder.

"Not again!" she said, listening to the roar outside and dreading the idea of taking another house ride to a faraway land known for its undatable men.

She wasn't sure how long they slid through the darkness (it was a very long hallway). She wasn't sure when the pungent aroma of dog poo wafted past her nostrils. She wasn't sure at what moment she flexed her feet and felt the mud-like consistency of Toto's crap smooshing between her toes. Rage and repulsion overtook her as she contemplated taking Toto outside, tossing him into the air, and cackling like a witch as the tornado sucked his smarty-face poopy-butt into its vortex.

But instead, she held Toto tighter and—once she'd finally stopped sliding—snatched the flashlight from the hall closet and raced, dung flinging from her bare feet, out the back door. The wind whipped the branches of the giant oak trees that towered over her, the flashlight's strip of yellow light bouncing as she ran toward the tornado shelter.

Suddenly the slanted streaks of rain stopped falling and a deafening roar filled Dorothy's ears. It was the roar of a train engine combined with a turbo jet. It was petrifying, but not as petrifying as the runny puppy poo underneath her toenails. She flung the shelter door open, leaped inside, and slammed it shut as a huge branch crashed nearby.

Dorothy and Toto huddled in safety on the cold concrete floor. The roar dissipated and rain started to fall again. She held Toto's trembling body. At one point he gazed up at her and whimpered.

And as she shined the flashlight on her dookie-covered toes, Dorothy was glad she hadn't sacrificed Toto to the tornado. She knew that if the house was still standing, she would need some bleach and a pedicure, STAT. She also knew she would spend the rest of the night cleaning her foot-shaped crap prints off the floors. She knew that there would be future accidents. But she didn't care.

The tornado passed over that night. It didn't touch down. But now, whenever the tornado sirens go off, Dorothy always, always, wears shoes.

"A house without a dog is not a home."

This motto might as well be emblazoned into the side of my family crest, embroidered on our pillows, and tattooed on our foreheads from birth. In my family, we're dog people whether we like it or not.

My grandmother likes to proclaim, "Never trust a man who dislikes children and dogs."

If that's the case, my sister Rebecca is suspect. Dangle an adorable baby with a peaches and cream complexion and pink smocked gown in front of her and she'll withdraw in horror.

"That's okay," she'll purse her glossy lips, readjusting her suit lapels, nostrils sucked in as if they detect the contagious scent of procreation, "I don't need to hold it."

But on the flip side, dangle a puppy in her face and she'll snatch it into a death grip, maul its head with kisses while gushing in her loudest, most babyish voice, "Who's the cutest dog in the world? You are!"

And then she'll demand that everyone around agree. Heaven help you if you don't.

Like I said, we're dog people. My family is the scariest, most aggressive, dog-sweater-buying, Christmas-postcard-printing, elaborate-name-tag-engraving group of dog lovers known to the South.

I'm no exception. I waited my whole life to have my very own dog.

Matt and I both grew up in dog-loving homes. It was a shared interest of ours from the beginning. Some couples bond over the fact that they both want to retire in the south of France by age forty. Some couples squeal with excitement when they discover they both want to have ten children. Some couples share a deep abiding love of hiking, working out at the gym, or playing the stock market.

Matt and I just wanted to buy a dog.

We drove an hour away to purchase our very first pet. They were advertised in the paper: MINIATURE PINSCHERS, $75.

Now, the cheap price tag for a breed dog should have been our first clue that the events about to unfold would not go as expected. The rural drive on bumpy roads lined with rebel-flag-flying four-wheelers should have been the second clue.

We parked on a dirt road in front of a quaint farmhouse with a large yard enclosed by a white picket fence. An elderly lady decked in a white apron with her hair pulled into a bun greeted us at the gate.

"Y'all here for the puppy?"

"Yes ma'am," I called, sidestepping a giant pile of horse manure.

She opened the gate as six dogs yapped and barked around her feet. "My name's Doris. Don't worry, they won't bite 'cha."

But being the dog lover that I am, I was still suspicious. Anyone versed in small dogs knows that they are always capable of biting—no matter what the owner tells you. Small dogs are perhaps more vicious than their larger counterparts. Big dogs that bite are usually just mean, but with smaller dogs it's a much more complex psychological situation. Due to their vast (and never to be underestimated) intelligence, they are perfectly aware of their small statures and globally inconsequential status; they realize that at any moment someone might punt kick them like a football. Therefore, when in fear, they bite. It's classic Scrappy-Doo syndrome.

Matt and I entered the yard with caution, eyeing the surrounding dogs for signs that our legs might soon be made into Swiss cheese. To our delight, we found that they jumped and wagged their small stub-like min-pin tails in happy greetings.

"Now . . . these are my breedin' dogs," Doris stated genially, patting her miniature pinschers on their heads. "For the life of me I can't remember which one is the mama, but there are two pups left out of the latest litter. They're over by the bushes."

And so we chose our dog. Or rather, Matt chose her. We caught our first glimpse as her behind disappeared into a patch of hosta.

"I like that one, let's pick her." Matt pointed to the invisible dog hiding in the foliage.

"I can't even see what she looks like!" I peered between the leaves, noting a pair of terrified, cartoonish eyes blinking back. I instantly thought of Jack and the expression that must have been on his face when he clambered up the beanstalk and caught sight of the horrendous man-devouring giant.

"Yep, that's the one," Matt stated resolutely. I watched, stunned into silence as Matt reached down and plucked the tiny, nondescript puppy from the bushes. She had short dark hair, her only defining feature a set of giant brown eyes lined with black eyelashes.

I examined Matt, totally befuddled by my normally passive "whatever you want is fine with me" husband choosing our first pet without so much as even consulting me.

"Fine. Do you want to name her too?" I needled sarcastically.

"Yes, I like the name Mabel. Let's name her Mabel."

And with that proclamation, Matt strode across the yard and handed Doris the cash.

"That'll be a right good dog for you young folks," she smiled. "These min-pins got plenty of energy."

Somewhere in the distance, behind the walls of the farmhouse, a monstrous chorus of dogs erupted. I glanced sideways to see numerous snarling mouths smashed against the glass door, saliva flinging into the air, the mini-blinds swinging wildly.

"Eh . . ." Doris waved her hand in the air nonchalantly. "Don't mind them. They's just my schnauzers that live inside. They're just a scad protective of me."

I returned my gaze to the door full of teeth and noses. I didn't know what a "scad" was, but the vibrating glass door looked like a fishbowl full of rabid Old Yellers. Even if I had been left out of the dog-choosing loop, at least we weren't taking one of those dogs home.

I moped all the way to the car, begrudgingly holding the puppy I'd dreamed of for so long yet had not been able to pick out nor name. But after a solid five seconds it was all water under the bridge. She shook and blinked up at me with an expression that pleaded, "Please, please, whatever you do, don't make me sleep alone."

It was all a ruse of course, the promise of her miniature pinscher heritage, her carefully crafted facade of fear and delicacy. She was not delicate. She was not afraid. And she was not, I repeat not, a miniature pinscher.

She carried on the charade for a couple of weeks. She was meek, quiet, and pitiful in her squatted attempts to potty outside, gazing up at me with giant lash-lined peepers. We listened, amused, when we heard her first bark, a surprisingly forceful "garrruuufff" that carried with it an Irish trill and a shocking amount of vibrato.

"Isn't that cute," we both remarked. We were blissfully unaware that soon (very soon, and for years to come) that bark would become our constant and never-wavering alarm signaling a variety of events:

- The mailman, a pedestrian, children, a squirrel, or a ghost daring to walk within fifty feet of our yard.

- Hunger at the appointed times of morning, mid-morning, afternoon, mid-afternoon, early evening, dinnertime, and bedtime.

- Any number of specific requests ranging from "scratch my armpits and do it now" to "woman you haven't paid me enough undivided attention within the last ten minutes so here, let me heft my toy into the air as a projectile weapon aimed for your face."

Shortly thereafter Mabel jumped from the floor onto my lap, and I bragged on her for her athletic prowess. While kissing the top of her head I noticed a new and strange development.

"Matt," I held her face upward with both hands, "get in here and look at this."

"What?" He ran into the room, his countenance oozing fatherly concern. "What's wrong? Is she sick?"

"No, but . . ." I positioned Mabel's face so he could get a better look.

"Huh, that's weird," he said, kneeling next to me.

We examined her carefully. It appeared she was growing a bushy set of . . . eyebrows.

"Do miniature pinschers have facial hair like that?" I pondered.

"No, no they don't," Matt said while carefully raising her head and pointing beneath her chin.

I gasped.

"They don't have beards either," he noted grimly, eyeing the small tuft of hair that had mysteriously sprouted from her chin.

"Oh my gosh!" The truth hit me instantly. "The fish bowl of Old Yellers!"

Matt stared at me blankly. "What?"

"The schnauzers inside Doris's house! Schnauzers have eyebrows and beards!"

We sat in stunned silence. We stared at our little impostor. She stared back at us.

"That would explain the eyelashes." Matt put his arm around me.

"And the cheap price! She's not a full-blood miniature pinscher at all. I bet the father was a schnauzer," I said.

Mabel perched before us, glancing back and forth, back and forth, giant eyes blinking like a bug.

"Do you think she'll be mean like those other dogs?" I sniffed and patted her head.

"No. We'll train her better than that," Matt assured me.

And train her we did. We walked her around a college campus to socialize her. We taught her to sit and stay and roll over with treats. When it came to potty training, she caught on immediately and hardly ever had accidents. We did the best we could.

In the process, there were a lot of casualties of war. She ate my favorite pair of red heels. She nibbled the leg of our dining table, the linoleum floor, the baseboards, the wood floors in the hallway, and Matt's *Silence of the Lambs* DVD.

And while Mabel's number one goal in life was to kill and eat any intruder in our house, she held a special place in her heart for family members. When greeted with the sight of my parents, Mabel liked to show her love by spinning in circles like a toy top. When my sisters knocked on the door, Mabel's vocal chords reached record heights as her intimidating bark morphed into glass-breaking screeches of delight. My uncles, cousins, and best friend Carrie were also inducted into the "Mabel's House of Love" club, each greeted with licks and butt-waggling hellos.

For everyone outside Mabel's circle of trust, however, there was only weeping and gnashing of teeth. Literally. She would bound on top of the couch, conquering its downy heights with her feet, squishing it into submission with her ever-widening behind as she mashed her face into the front window, teeth clattering against the glass as a warning to whatever trespasser dared ring the front doorbell.

Mabel timed her window attacks with careful precision. Her internal clock was set on high alert for certain times during the day and week. The mailman's visits were expected, even relished, every day at approximately 10:00. She knew innately when the garbage truck would make an appearance on Friday mornings. She would quiver in excitement and expectation, waiting for the moment she could open the floodgates and unleash her shrieking hysteria at the front window. But it wasn't too long before her rage sessions found a new target: Angela.

After an entire summer of commuting to work in separate vehicles, it dawned on Angela and me that we lived a mere five miles from each other and it made economic sense to carpool. (Okay, in truth, economics had nothing to do with it. We just liked to gab.)

The first day Angela picked me up she pulled into the driveway and Mabel clambered on top of our couch, which at this stage of its life looked like the Stay Puft Marshmallow Man after he'd gone twelve rounds with Mike Tyson and a ref who allowed excessive ear biting. It was dimpled with golf ball–like divots, not unlike the burgeoning cellulite on the back of my legs.

I gathered my purse and umbrella, swatting at Mabel as I exited the house, "Shut up!" She dodged the swat and continued to shriek at Angela, stomping her hind legs for emphasis.

I went out, shutting the door swiftly before Mabel had a chance to squish her angry, snorting nose through the crack and continue her harassment.

As I got into Angela's car, I began to apologize.

"Sorry about that. Her name is Mabel, and don't be offended. She literally hates everyone."

Angela smiled at the front window just as Mabel kamikaze-attacked the glass with her teeth. "Don't worry. Remember, I have dogs. I'm well acquainted with animal quirks."

I smiled, appreciative of Angela's kind assessment of Mabel's terroristic threats as "quirks." "Yeah, well, she's absolutely ruined my couch. You should see it."

It's often said that people resemble their pets, or vice versa. If I were a vain woman I would deny this fact to the death since Mabel desperately needs a diet for her rotund backside and a daily regime of anti-anxiety medication. But denying our similarities would do no good in light of the fact that she and I are doggy-human soul mates.

Do we pick animals that reflect us? Or do animals mesh so well into our lives that they mimic our dispositions and appearances? It's impossible to prove one way or the other, but when it came to Angela, her husband Bryan, and their two dogs, there was never a clearer case of animal-owner symmetry.

Angela and Bryan had been happily married almost ten years. Their dogs, Sabi and Gerard, were the most well-cared for, well-loved animals to ever sleep on a king-size bed at night. They also perfectly reflected Angela and Bryan's symbiotic relationship.

Sabi was a Shiba Inu, a breed of dog that looks like a small graceful fox. Her tiny eyes were piercing, and I often felt like I was making eye contact with an incredibly intelligent rocket scientist trapped in an animal's body. Sabi examined all new people like bugs under the microscope, but once she decided Matt and I were suitable human beings, her loyalty was unwavering.

Gerard was a large boxer with a dark reverse brindle coat, but his giant head and massive teeth were misleading. He looked like he was capable of killing anything in sight, when in truth, he really just wanted to mash his gigantic body into visitors' laps and cover their faces with happy drooly greetings. He galloped merrily all over the neighborhood, straining at the end of his leash. The world was his playground, a new adventure around every corner.

Watching these two polar opposite canines coexist was nothing less than a comic sideshow. Gerard jumped joyfully at the sight of Sabi; covering her face in kisses as she stood stoically, appreciative of his zest for life. When Sabi spotted an intruder in their front yard she barked and yipped at the front window. Gerard stood behind her, every muscle rigid, totally silent, uncharacteristically intimidating. She made the noise, but it was clear—happy demeanor or no—Gerard was ready to do battle with anyone who threatened her safety.

It was no different with Angela and Bryan.

Bryan was a towering police officer, an all-around happy man who had never met a stranger. Angela was ladylike, poised, and loyal. He was genial, she was introspective. It was obvious to everyone that they, like their pets, were two sides of a very happy coin.

For months our rides to work were pleasant and we passed the time chatting and listening to music. What had once been a lonely and boring commute filled with stalled traffic and blaring horns became enjoyable as we discussed literature and office drama. One morning, as we sipped our coffees and waited while traffic stacked up downtown, I noticed Angela was very quiet.

"Is anything wrong?" I asked.

"I went to the doctor a few days ago," she mentioned casually.

"Why? Are you feeling all right?"

"Yes, I'm feeling just fine. But I found a knot on my arm."

She extended her arm so I could feel the long, low knot on the underside of her forearm.

"Why didn't you tell me?" I was surprised she'd already been to the doctor.

Angela swept her hand in the air, "There's really no need for anyone to worry unduly. The doctor should get back to me today."

I frowned. The idea of keeping my cards close to my chest was a foreign one. I had no filter when it came to worries and concerns.

"I'm sure it's just a cyst," I said.

"That's what Bryan said," she nodded.

I felt better, knowing Bryan shared my opinion.

Angela and I arrived at work fifteen minutes late and in a panic. We ran through the front doors and headed toward our respective departments. The second I walked into my office I discovered four new voicemails, a stack of packages that required signing for, and a boss in need of caffeine. I bustled about, brewing coffee and adjusting the sign on my desk that read: I HAVE FLYING MONKEYS AND I'M NOT AFRAID TO USE THEM.

Shortly before noon, everything changed.

A coworker rushed across the hallway and motioned for me.

"You better get in there," she pointed at Angela's door.

I quickly crossed the hallway and pushed the door open.

Angela was sitting on the floor behind her desk, her arms wrapped around her knees. She looked up at me, tears streaming down her face.

"It's cancer. The doctor said the lump in my arm is cancer." Her voice cracked beneath the strain of the diagnosis. She was thirty-one years old.

When someone says "I have cancer" it means a lot of things.

"My hair will fall out and people are going to stare at me."

"Everyone around me is healthy and going to live, I'm totally alone."

"I'm going to hurt and be sick. Oh God, I don't want to be in pain."

"I could die."

And while it's a multifaceted statement, it's also a question.

"Do you think I'll make it?"

"What should I do?"

"Do you know anyone who's survived?"

"What really happens when we die?"

As I stood there, looking down at her tear-stained face, I was utterly blindsided. I realized that up until that point, life had treated me with kid gloves. I'd never had to face anything harder than a bounced check or gallbladder surgery. It was my turn to step up to the plate, to be strong. It turned out to be a swing and a miss.

What I said to her, my response at that moment, is something that causes me physical pain to this day.

"Oh, Ang. I'm so sorry . . . I'll pray for you."

That shouldn't be an empty statement. Telling someone you'll pray for them should be the highest form of love and encouragement on Earth. But I think we all know that most of the time, it's what you say because you don't know what else to fill the air with. It's a verbal scapegoat. I pulled the fail-safe lever and out of my mouth tumbled an insulting little parachute, perhaps the most clichéd phrase in the book.

As I said it, as the word "pray" slipped past my lips, I realized how lame it must have sounded to her. I'd never prayed for anything that important before. Oh sure, I'd prayed for sick people, people whose names I knew through a friend of a friend. I'd prayed that the closing on our house wouldn't fall through. I'd prayed for Matt to have a safe business trip and for my mom to win an art show. I'd even prayed that God would help me find an affordable dining room set. But when it came to the biggies—cancer, spiritual paths, religious questions—I had bubkes. And if I'd never prayed for anything big, had I ever really prayed? And if I hadn't prayed, did God even know who I was?

But as soon as those thoughts filled my head like water rushing into a lock system, I pushed them away. I shoved them back into the recesses of my brain and slammed the door shut. It was all too much to process. And so, feeling totally inadequate and unable to comfort or help or even pray, I sat down on Angela's office floor. I held her hand and the clock on the wall ticked loudly while she continued to cry.

Our commutes became quiet ones. Days passed. Angela didn't say much and I didn't ask any questions. We didn't talk about gardening. We didn't talk about the fun we'd had over the summer. We didn't mention the cancer. For some quiet people it's important to break down the barriers, to scale the heights of their privacy fences and initiate conversation about the hard things. But I knew innately that somehow, when she was ready to talk, Angela would.

"Is there anything I can do?" I asked one day.

"No, but if I think of anything I'll let you know," was her polite yet firm response that subtly let me know she wasn't ready to face it.

A week later we arrived back at my house after a long day at work. The evening had turned purple and chilly. I could smell wood smoke in the air.

"Have a good night, Ang."

"Actually," she leaned over, looking up at the house, "I'd like to meet Mabel."

I sucked air through my teeth, "Ehhh . . . I'm not so sure that's a good idea."

"Why, will she bite me?"

I paused, contemplating the question. Mabel had actually never bitten anyone. She usually just circled people like a maniacal hedgehog, screaming and snarling until they retreated in fear.

"No, but, it's just, she's just . . . unpleasant."

"I love dogs," Angela answered resolutely as she exited the car and headed for the front porch.

Mabel was already at her front window perch clanking against the glass, which rendered a sound similar to teeth on a fork. I unlatched the door and Angela walked inside.

Mabel jumped from the couch, her screaming barks soaring to levels ambulances would envy. And then, as she reached Angela, she stopped. She began to sniff Angela's shoes and legs. Mabel's tail twirled in its typical helicopter fashion and she squealed happily.

Angela kneeled down, petting Mabel's head and scratching behind her ears. "See, I told you Liz. I love dogs."

I watched, dumbfounded, as the terror of our street and Angela forged an instant friendship.

Mabel leaped up at Angela, slurping her on the lips. Angela just laughed, wiping her mouth with her sleeve, "Yes, I like you too. I do believe your mother has made you out to be a bigger monster than you truly are."

"I don't understand. She's never warmed up to anyone so fast," I said.

Angela turned toward the couch, "Goodness . . . she really is ruining that! It looks like she's crushing it to death."

I nodded, my mouth still agape. "I can't believe she's being this nice to you. You don't understand, other than my parents and sisters she really doesn't do this . . ."

Angela scratched Mabel again. "I suspect she knew I needed a friend today."

I nodded, baffled and pleased as Mabel once again tried to lick Angela in the mouth. If ever there was a person that didn't need to be shrieked at, it was Angela.

"It all starts next week. There'll be radiation, surgery, and chemotherapy," she said, pulling Mabel onto her lap. "This has always been my greatest fear you know. Cancer." She smiled tightly, dignity buoying her upward at a moment when most people, myself included, would have dissolved into tears.

"My stepfather died of lung cancer," she drew a deep breath. "It was horrible. I've seen what cancer does. Slowly, little by little, it carves all your dignity away. Before you know it, you don't know who you are anymore. You cease to be you."

I sat quietly for a moment and then cleared my throat. "What can I do?"

She continued to smile and scratch Mabel's face. "You're doing it." She stood up. "Thank you for letting me visit with your dog."

"Anytime, Ang."

And with that she left. Mabel leaped back onto the dying couch, stomping her feet and whimpering as she watched

Angela walk to her car. The lump in my throat was suffocating. I didn't know what she meant by "you're doing it." I wasn't doing anything but standing around with my hands in my pockets, kicking at rocks like a useless imbecile while she faced cancer.

"Mabel, get off the couch."

Mabel turned and looked me squarely in the eye, comprehending every word, turned around three times, and took roost in the back cushion that looked like an eighty-year-old woman who had forgotten to wear her bra.

I've always looked upon parents who didn't spank their children with a smidge of disdain. My parents spanked me, my aunts and uncles spanked my cousins, and my grandmother still threatens to spank my sixty-year-old mother. I once had a friend who gazed lovingly at her three-year-old trying to hold a cat up by its tail while she cooed, "I just can't seem to bring myself to spank little Billy. I just don't have it in my heart." I found myself stifling snorts of supremacy and condemnation. I referred to people like that as "Big Fat Wiener Parents."

I always believed that if I ever chose to have children, they would be spanked and often. They would wear matching uniforms and when I (just like Captain Von Trapp) would blow a whistle, they would salute and march.

And yet, as I gazed at my overweight dog, secure and snug and in total defiance of my order to get off the couch, I began to see the emptiness of my previous pro-spanking blustering. How would I ever be able to make a child tremble in absolute obedience when I couldn't even bring myself to roll up a newspaper and spank Mabel?

Perhaps I was not so tough. Perhaps I was the Big Fat Wiener Parent.

"Mabel, get off the couch."

Mabel closed her eyes, sighing deeply as she snuggled further into the cushions.

But then again, Mabel had done a good thing. She had welcomed Angela. She had, in some sort of dog-way, sensed that Angela was good and trustworthy. She had, perhaps, sensed that Angela didn't need to be threatened or barked at. Angela needed love. Angela needed comfort.

I glanced out the window, watching Angela drive away. I might not know what needed to be done. I might not possess Mabel's canine ability to comfort, but if dogs teach us anything in this life, they teach us the meaning of loyalty. And while I wasn't sure what Angela needed, I was determined to stand next to her no matter what was coming. After all, she would do the same for me.

Chapter 4

Pride, Prejudice, and Personal Possessions

Mr. Bennet stroked his long white mustache as he listened to the kerfuffle taking place outside the door in the hallway.

"Lizzie! You promised you would loan me your floral shawl!"

"So what? I lied."

"But you promised!"

"Knock it off, you're not getting it."

"Motherrrrrrr!"

Mr. Bennet ducked his head and leaned back in his tufted brown leather chair. He folded his hands across his belly and smiled as he listened to the sound of his scuffling daughters drift farther and farther away to the other end of the house.

His gaze drifted around the room, a small library stacked high with books and paintings. A wall of open windows allowed a fall breeze to ruffle the papers on his desk. A fireplace behind him crackled cozily, and his prized possessions rested on the stone mantle. It was a sea of plaid, brown leather, and wide-planked floors, a tiny kingdom all his own with magical powers to repel all things pink and feminine. His daughters dubbed it "Mr. Bennet's Man Cave."

Without warning, the tall oak door swung open and Mrs. Bennet bustled inside angrily.

Mrs. Bennet had, at one time in her life, been very attractive. She had been tiny and petite with glistening brunette curls and a gay laugh that lit up the sun. But five daughters and five thousand cheesecakes later, her body had ballooned and her disposition curdled. It wasn't that Mr. Bennet minded her healthy figure; he actually thought her waddle was cute. It was her incessant nagging that drove him into emotional paralysis.

"Did you not hear what was happening out there?"

Mr. Bennet ducked his head again, eyeing a loose button on his jacket. He often feared that if he looked directly at his wife at her angriest, she might sprout snakes from her head and turn him into a big chunk of stone with a mustache.

"All you do is hide in here," she continued, eyeing the precariously stacked books on the side table nearest her. She reached out and picked up a magnifying glass and a wilted ivy plant. "Ugh. I think it's time we redecorated this room. Just look at the rug, it looks like someone brought it over from India in the Middle Ages."

And then, something strange began to happen. Mr. Bennet peered past his wife and into the formal living room across the hall. It was awash in pink glass lanterns and doilies stretched on anything that could pass for furniture. The drapes were gold with baby blue birds, carnations, and angels with harps. The floor was covered in at least fifteen different rugs, all in various shades of pink, mauve, and purple. Mr. Bennet felt a strange rumbling in his stomach, not the usual kind that resulted in an aroma of public embarrassment, but the kind that spread upwards like a hot flame.

Suddenly, for the first time in thirty years, Mr. Bennet was good and mad.

"Mrs. Bennet." He rose quickly, gripping the sides of his oak desk, his face darkening to a deep shade of red. "This is the only room I can claim as my own in this entire house. A house filled with female servants, five daughters, you, and your lady Bunco group."

"Well, pardon me," Mrs. Bennet stammered huffily, her mind racing to remember the last time her spouse was angry. She couldn't recall a single incident, not even the time when the neighbor accidentally killed their favorite cow, Moo-Face.

"Well, nothing!" Mr. Bennet growled and slammed a book on the table for emphasis. "You're going to redecorate my room? Fine, then I'm going to redecorate yours."

He whirled around, scooped a large framed object from his mantle, jammed a pipe in his mouth, and stomped out of the room.

Mrs. Bennet fluttered behind him nervously. "There's no need to throw a fit of this magnitude. I was merely mentioning that your library could use some sprucing up . . ."

Mr. Bennet marched directly to the marble fireplace and, pushing aside her dainty porcelain figurines, positioned the framed piece directly in front of Great Aunt Martha's wigged portrait.

"Good heavens!" Mrs. Bennet gasped and clutched the sofa back for support.

The framed piece that Mr. Bennet had brought forth from the library was something passed down from his father: a giant, clunky, scrap-lumber-framed antique flyer. It read:

WILLIE FITZPATRICK
1802 SOUTH LONDON BOXING CHAMPION
SPONSORED BY BIG BELLY BEER

Etched into the corners of the flyer were dancing girls, their bare legs kicking out from under ruffled skirts. On every third girl there was a glimpse of underwear.

Mrs. Bennet briefly pondered faking a swooning session, but as she gazed into her husband's uncharacteristically determined face, she realized it was useless.

"You know I hate that thing! Your father gave it to you just to spite me!" she yelled.

"Earnestine, if you're going to defile my Man Cave with lace curtains and tea cups, then this is staying right here."

And suddenly Mrs. Bennet realized the value of her husband's man space. It was the repository for all the things she hated. It contained hundreds of dusty books she would have preferred to donate to the Troubled Girls Foundation. And scattered around the stiff, lodge-like furniture were horrendous trinkets ranging from novelty pipes to beer-can openers shaped like naked ladies. She realized that if Mr. Bennet's Man Cave ceased to be, the door would fly open and all his unsightly and unwomanly belongings would invade the rest of the house. Manliness and bad taste would encroach on her carefully constructed world of gilded girldom.

"Fine." She held her nose in the air. "I won't do a thing to your sacred Man Cave. It's all yours."

Mr. Bennet nodded curtly, a smile creeping into the corners of his mouth. He plucked his boxing flyer from the mantle and refrained from pulling a few air punches of victory. Crossing the hall, he drew a deep breath of man room air (the combined scent of old socks and pine) and shut the door behind him.

"Do you know what truly chaps my hide?" Angela stated loudly, at the exact moment I sipped a giant mouthful of hot tea.

I snorted in surprise, which resulted in an embarrassing combination of snot and tea dribbling down the front of my face. It was lunchtime and Angela and I were sitting on a narrow park bench tucked into a wooded corner, the trees above us covered in yellow leaves.

Hearing Angela combine the words "chap" and "hide" in the same sentence was as unexpected as Margaret Thatcher yelling at Parliament, "You gents have done torn your drawers with me!"

But I was learning more and more that Angela was a woman of many layers. On the surface she was poised, totally refined, and somewhat reserved with people she didn't know very well. But underneath lay a loyal friend who shocked me into laughing on a daily basis.

My first inkling that Angela was not all ladylike lace and gloves was my discovery of her tattoo. After work one day, while she was putting on her sweater, I noticed some color on her shoulder, just above her shirt collar.

"Do you have . . . a . . . ?" I couldn't even finish the sentence, it seemed so improbable.

"A tattoo?" Angela asked, gathering her purse and keys. "Yes. A rather large one."

I blinked several times, shocked. The idea of Angela, who collected English teacups and possessed a covet-worthy IQ, having a massive tattoo was similar to finding out the pope had a poker table in his bedroom, or that Oprah dipped snuff in the privacy of her lush high-rise penthouse.

"I drew the fox myself and had an artist tattoo me several years ago. Foxes are my favorite animal, you know. Such elusive creatures," she responded.

As odd as the tattoo seemed then, over time I realized that Angela was a woman who could never be completely figured out. So while I shouldn't have been surprised that she could fling the phrase "chaps my hide" around as well as the next gun-toting Arkansan, it still took me by surprise.

"No," I laughed. "I do not know what chaps your hide. But do tell."

"Disney princesses." She shook her head in disgust. "I was shopping for a present for my niece, Evelyn, at the store last night and overheard the most appalling mother-daughter conversation. The daughter said, 'Mommy, am I just like a Disney princess?' And the mother responded, 'Of course honey, you're beautiful and have pretty hair.' The daughter—who wasn't more than four or five—flipped her ponytail over her shoulder and said, 'Yes. I am. And one day I will have a boyfriend just like Prince Eric.' Liz, I nearly vomited."

I grinned.

"And I stood there thinking about how the Disney princesses have absolutely no personality whatsoever. They're as flat and uninteresting as a piece of cardboard. The only interesting female characters are the evil queens. What does that say about our society?"

I shrugged, settling back into the park bench, thoroughly enjoying her rant.

"I'll tell you what it means. It means I'd rather Evelyn idealize Maleficent from *Sleeping Beauty* than fantasize about lying around waiting for a man to kiss her so she can begin her life." Angela paused, noticing my amused expression. "What, you don't agree?"

"No, totally I agree," I laughed. "And don't worry; no one would ever confuse you with a Disney princess. I've seen you in action with Felicia. You could totally be Maleficent."

She sniffed and straightened her sweater, "Thank you."

Our conversation shifted back to our usual lunchtime topic: writing. Angela and I were both working on stories, which had quickly expanded into hundreds of pages of ideas.

I'd been writing stories since I was old enough to fold over notebook paper and draw stick figures. Characters, ideas, even simple words woke me up in the middle of the night and distracted me during work meetings. I was driven to write.

"Do you think our publishers would let us go on a book tour together?" I joked.

Angela smiled. "Anything is possible. But for all your decorating endeavors and scheming, I'm quite surprised you haven't carved out a library for yourself."

Angela's comment took me by surprise; I put aside my decorating magazine. "What are you talking about?"

"I'm just merely commenting on the fact that you should have a room of your own. A place to shut the door and write. Why don't you create a room like that? After all, Ms. Woolf said it best: 'A woman must have money and a room of her own if she is to write fiction.'"

It was true. I'd spent hours perusing Craigslist for a Mabel-proof couch. I'd foraged flea markets and antique malls for paintable side tables, shutters to hang in the dining room, and vintage pottery to display in the kitchen. And yet I was still doing most of my writing on an ancient computer atop a scratched science table from an old country school.

Angela had created her own retreat long ago by laying claim to a tiny spare bedroom. She pinned a picture of Alice's White Rabbit on the front door and referred to the small book-lined room as "The Rabbit Hole." She wrote, did crafts, and read in the late afternoon sunlight that flooded through the window.

"You could be right. I need a room."

Angela nodded, "Of course I am. How can you pen a great adventure saga or a sweeping romance if you're propped up in the dining room while Mabel tosses her toys at you? After all, Matt has his den. It just stands to reason you deserve a room for writing."

I watched her with admiration. With everything going on in her life, she still had the generosity and clarity to help me see what I needed to get my life together. She was dealing with her diagnosis remarkably well. She made phone calls to doctors and nurses, scheduling tests, chemo, and surgery with the same efficiency with which she scheduled meetings at work. The official diagnosis was "undifferentiated sarcoma." Angela responded by saying, "I do so hate to be ordinary; it makes sense I'd end up with a zebra disease instead of a regular old horse. I shall name my tumor Fred. After all, every archenemy needs a name."

A cold breeze blew leaves into the air, a gust of yellow spiraling around us. She shivered and pulled her sweater closer. Her jawline was sharp and angled from weight loss. She adjusted the emerald green scarf covering her head. Her hair was gone. The day she'd shaved it all off she'd joked, "I always wanted to be Jo March and now I am. My one beauty is gone."

But that couldn't have been further from the truth. To those who loved her, she was more beautiful than ever.

I took another bite of my sandwich and nodded, "Yep. I need an office."

Angela shook her head sternly. "Not an office, a library. Bob Cratchit worked in an office. Jane Austen wrote in a library."

"Did she? I thought Jane Austen wrote on a tiny table in the corner of . . ."

My voice trailed off as I caught a glimpse of Angela's expression. Our park bench was to be a no-nonsense zone. My mission was clear. She intended I have a room of my own. A library for a writer, not an office for a drone.

We got up and walked back to our office building. We didn't work in the best of neighborhoods, so when we saw a homeless woman pushing her grocery cart toward us, her entire body covered in layers of filthy clothing and her matted gray hair covering most of her face, we weren't surprised.

I tend to be a suspicious person by nature. I've always chalked it up to the fact that I've watched every single crime melodrama on cable television. Where most people pass by a family on the side of the road changing a flat tire and think, "I should help," I see a complex crime-ring scam devised to steal my purse or stuff me in a trunk. And where most people would look at a homeless woman and see an unfortunate soul, I saw a crazed psycho killer.

Angela cleared her throat and addressed the woman directly.

"Excuse me ma'am, have you eaten today?"

The woman blinked at Angela a few times, her eyes blurry and mouth moving silently in an attempted response.

Angela reached out and put some money into her hand, "Here, take this and get something to eat."

The homeless woman stared blankly into her palm for a few moments.

"Is there anything else I can do for you?" Angela leaned in, undaunted by the woman's filthy clothes and slightly unhinged expression.

The woman eyed her for a moment, and then pointed toward Angela's scarf-covered head. "Sick?" she croaked.

Angela paused for a moment.

"Yes. Sick. But getting better."

The woman gave a half smile and pocketed the money deep within the folds of her clothing. She pointed to herself several times and then whispered, "Me too. Sick, but getting better."

We watched her shuffle away, the wheels of her grocery cart whirring down the street. I knew deep in my heart that I would have never spoken to the homeless woman. I would never have asked her if she'd eaten, would never have given her money. I would have looked at the ground and walked quickly past.

I cleared my throat, "You're a good person."

"For heavens sake, Liz. I gave the woman a few dollars. It doesn't exactly make me the Dalai Lama."

"No, but it does make me feel guilty."

She rolled her eyes and then grinned, "Guilt is for suckers."

We walked for a few moments in silence before Angela spoke up, "Now, how about your library? Can I expect you'll start making progress soon?"

I cleared my throat, "Tomorrow is trash day. I'll drive around the neighborhood and see if I can find some free furniture for the office—I mean, library."

She nodded again in approval, reaching out to catch a leaf floating past her face. "I think that's a marvelous idea. After all, a poached egg isn't poached unless it's stolen from the forest in the dead of night."

"Is that Shakespeare?"

"No," she grinned. "Roald Dahl. And I'm fairly sure that quote sums up why you love found furniture so much."

I began making a mental list. First I would need to clean the spare bedroom. Then I would consult my stacks of magazines for decorating inspiration. Why hadn't I thought of this before? After all, Anne Shirley must have had a study in Green Gables. It was probably a small room, tucked away at the back of the house with floor-to-ceiling bookshelves, a dainty desk, and a large window overlooking a garden flourishing with tomatoes and strawberries.

I pondered the size of our house. Taking over an entire room for the pursuit of one solitary endeavor is no small thing when you're dealing with 1,400 square feet and tiny closets. And yet, Angela had a point. If Matt had a Man Cave, a dark place designed to block out sunlight and blast *Star Wars* in surround sound, wasn't I allowed a space of my own as well?

The creation of the Man Cave was an event that marked an epic turning point in the health of our marriage. Men come into marriage carrying all kinds of baggage. Some tote along a passionate fishing hobby. Some play pool with their friends, some hunt, and others play video games. Some men tread to the altar slowly, laden with baggage as they refuse to relinquish old football jerseys, taxidermy deer heads, or their grandfather's spittoon. Some men carry along years of black-book keeping, obsessions with baseball cards, and an affinity for belching the alphabet or their true love's full name.

My husband, however, came to our marital altar with only one serious burr that would eventually embed itself in my backside, and that burr's name was Chuck.

We had begun our marriage in a small rented house just a block from our college campus. In the beginning we didn't have much in the way of material possessions. We owned a peach-and-country-blue plaid couch, a lopsided navy recliner, and a bed from Craigslist. And while dowries are a thing of the past, we each brought our own set of household supplies to our new home.

I brought two turquoise lamps, a striped rug, and a complete set of my grandmother's rose-patterned china. Matt brought a beanbag, a body pillow with a duct-taped hole, movie memorabilia, and a giant plastic Buddha named Chuck.

My mother was quick to point out that in the decor-world "beggars can't be choosers," but I didn't feel it was fair to apply this logic to Chuck.

Chuck stood knee high and was made of sturdy plastic with a faux-marble finish. Chuck was, in my opinion, the most horrible, heinous, and loathsome lump of manufactured material ever to drift from the shores of China. Do not mistake my distaste for Chuck. If Matt had been a Buddhist, I would have suffered Chuck's presence in silence, or perhaps suggested we buy a statelier, more high-end statue. But great lover of peace that he was, Matt was not a Buddhist.

Matt's love for Chuck ran deep. Chuck was more than just a mold-colored statue bought at the local flea market. Chuck had stood loyally in Matt's dorm room for three years overseeing many hours of pizza eating, video game playing, and pranking. Chuck was present for Matt's poker victories, study sessions, and midnight movie marathons. Chuck was the mascot for Matt's entire carefree college experience wrapped up in one ugly die-cast object.

I felt a deep conviction that Chuck had no place in my living room. I also felt assured with the faith of the saints that the *Empire Strikes Back* poster over the fireplace mantle was askew and did nothing for the room. I was certain that Matt's particle board computer desk perfectly resembled mission control on the *Star Trek* Enterprise. His Elvis clock raised my hackles with every swing of its plastic jointed hips. But none of these items lit the flame of self-righteous indignation in my soul like Chuck's cocky green expression as he taunted me from across the room.

In short, I hated Chuck.

I began to chafe under the decor constrictions after a few weeks of marriage. The white painted furniture I wanted for the living room did not match the fake-glossy-oak-veneer of the computer desk. A 1920s reproduction cat clock was far more suited to our little cottage rental than the Elvis clock and its gyrating pelvis. And when I suggested that we replace Matt's hole-riddled-duct-taped body pillow I was answered with a raised eyebrow and, "Why? That duct tape even holds up when I wash it."

But more than anything, I needed an exit strategy for Chuck. If necessary, I could break the computer and subsequently get rid of the computer desk. I could even "accidentally" knock Elvis from the wall and relegate the *Empire Strikes Back* poster to our bedroom. Under the bed.

But finding a way for Chuck's early demise stumped me.

My first effort involved edging Chuck farther and farther to the outskirts of the living room.

It was the night of our first party as a married couple and I cleaned the house. I buzzed around the living room as Chuck watched, dead center on the fireplace hearth, mocking my attempts to make the room look better. I glanced into the kitchen to see if Matt was looking and deftly picked Chuck up by his plastic head and hid him behind the couch.

I've never been passive-aggressive by nature. Ask anyone who knows me, or better yet, ask Matt and he'll tell you I'm a confronter, a metaphorical pimple popper. But somehow, when it came to Chuck, I intuitively knew to be quiet and move in the shadows as opposed to doing what I really wanted, which was to test Chuck's flame retardant abilities.

The couples arrived, pizza was plated, and Matt fired up a movie. It was exhilarating to host a party using our coral

Fiestaware wedding dishes. It was exciting to get suggestions on where to buy an affordable couch and what types of curtain rods the other wives preferred. And best of all, it was all done Chuck-free. I didn't even mind the knowledge that he was lurking behind the couch like a deranged toddler hidden from proper society.

After the guests left, Matt and I cleaned up. It was a comforting feeling, windows open, summer mockingbirds chirping in the trees outside. I felt truly married, as if we'd been that way for years, puttering around our little rented cottage, scraping plates and blowing out candles.

It was peaceful and lovely, that is, until Chuck tossed himself into the mix.

"Hey, what's he doing back here?" Matt leaned over the couch, resurrecting Chuck from the dead.

I felt my bottom jaw jut out defensively. "I put him there for the party. You know, so he wouldn't be in the way."

Matt frowned. "He wasn't in the way by the fireplace."

I took a deep breath and tried to remember my passive-aggressive plans. I tried to tell myself to live to fight another day. But I couldn't help it.

"Matt. That thing is ugly."

Matt held Chuck close to his bosom. "No. He. Is. Not."

"Okay, maybe he wasn't ugly in the dorms. He was cool there. But here, in this house, in the grown-up world . . . he's revolting."

And here it was. The truth was coming forth like projectile vomit.

I took a deep breath. "I'd really love it if we could just find a new home for Chuck . . ."

Matt's mouth gaped in horror.

". . . like the city dump."

"Hey! Did I say a thing when you brought home those awful rose dishes? No!"

"You mean my grandmother's china? I think that's a little different."

"No it isn't. At least Chuck is cool. That china makes me feel like I need a pacemaker, suspenders, and a Studebaker before I can be old enough to eat off of it."

I gritted my teeth, glaring at Chuck. This was his fault.

"I cannot believe we're having our first fight over that stupid thing."

"This isn't our first fight." Matt clutched Chuck even tighter, as if I was going to spring a Gumby arm across the room and sling him out the window. "Our first fight was about washing hands."

"Oh yes, how could I forget the time you told me not to wash my hands so much?"

"Germs are good for you."

"Sure. Despite the fact that the mere act of hand washing could have prevented the plagues, germs are good for us."

"Listen, I'm not telling you to lick a dollar bill or anything, but yes. Germs build up your immunity."

At this point I threw my hands in the air in surrender. I was so confused I could barely remember my initial argument for evicting Chuck, not to mention I was suddenly struck with an urge to scour my hands with soap and boiling water. Later in our marriage I would become wise to Matt's fighting strategy.

It was the husband fighting equivalent of rope-a-dope.

And so Chuck was replaced on the hearth, once again victorious over me. I simmered over it for the next few days until one pleasant afternoon when I was at home alone, the windows flung open as cheerful sunshine flooded the house. Soft French music played in the background, laundry hummed peacefully in the washer, and I was miserable, overwrought with hatred for Chuck.

After all, my own father never hung his deer antlers next to my mother's paintings. He never planted his books and tools and fishing poles on the hearth of the fireplace. I never dined with my grandfather's antique musket on the dining room table or dad's shoe shine material on the kitchen countertop. My father had the good taste to relegate his belongings to a room in the basement. Why should I suffer the abominable Chuck when I grew up in a house free of man trappings?

And at that moment I had an epiphany.

I strode down the tiny hallway and flung open the guest room door. It was a small room, with big windows. The closet housed Matt's clothes, which really meant the floor housed Matt's clothes. This in turn meant I'd long ago learned to call this room a lost cause in the fight for domestic spaces.

Why not exile all the things I hated, namely Chuck, to their own private island of Elba? I set about my mission, hands flying, propelling objects into the small room. I yanked the *Empire Strikes Back* poster from the mantle, while juggling an armful of movie memorabilia. I felt excitement brewing in my bosom as I wrenched apart his computer desk, reassembling it within the dark recesses of the spare room.

And saving the best for last, I picked up Chuck by his bald head and hefted him into a corner in his new home, slamming the door behind me. I felt free, emancipated. I felt as if I'd had the best haircut of my life, lost ten pounds, *and* won a trip to Jamaica. I was free of Chuck.

The clock ticked slowly and the sun's shadows grew long through the windows. I dusted and rearranged, reveling in my new freedom to decorate as I saw fit. But somewhere in the recesses of my brain, worry flickered.

What if Matt didn't like the new arrangement? What if his ego was bruised when he realized the depth of my hatred for his man accessories?

I heard his key turn in the lock and stood to face him.

"Hey," he said, dropping his backpack by the door and smiling at me. Slowly, the smile faded as he scanned the room. "What happened in here?"

"Well . . ." I started slowly.

"Where's my poster? My desk? My computer?" Panic filled Matt's eyes as his head whipped from side to side. "What have you done with Chuck?"

"Listen . . ." I held up my hands peaceably. "I have something to show you."

Matt looked at me much like Samson must have looked at Delilah the first time he caught her eyeing his long locks. Despite his reservations he took my outstretched hand, and let me lead him down the hallway.

"Now, don't be mad. But, I put all your things in the guest room." I opened the door.

Matt stood motionless for several moments, his face unreadable as I inspected it for warning signs of an explosion or impending divorce. Slowly, a smile dimpled his cheek.

"It's my very own room?" he marveled.

"Yep, you can do whatever you want in here."

"Wow . . ." he gushed, glassy eyed, awed by the prospect of being master of his very own universe, a universe that measured nine by nine feet.

"Just one restriction," I held up a finger. "No more man decorations in the rest of the house."

"Got it," Matt agreed, elated. "I can't believe it. It's like my very own Man Cave."

I smiled, pleased that he had accepted my arrangement without a fuss, pleased that he had not detected the ulterior motives born of my deep-seated hatred for Chuck.

And now I preach the necessities of the Man Cave Theory. While most women find the idea of losing an entire room repugnant, I feel the benefits outweigh the sacrifices. I back this up with seven key points:

1. The relief of not having to hang a *Rocky* poster in your formal living room will knock five points off your blood pressure.

2. The glow of a Pabst Blue Ribbon neon sign won't blind your dinner guests as it blinks above your dining room buffet.

3. You'll avoid the teeth rattling effect of surround sound as your husband constantly replays action scenes involving the helicopters in *Apocalypse Now,* clasps his hands, and gushes, "Seriously, listen to how great this sounds!"

4. It's an out of the way place to hide his complete set of *Police Academy* movies.

5. You won't be bothered with a fifty-two-inch TV perched precariously on top of the vintage buffet that you painstakingly sanded and painted kelly green to match the throw pillows on the couch.

6. You'll never again have to stare at your own personal Chuck, be it a taxidermy raccoon from your spouse's great-uncle or a bedpan once used during his fraternity's hazing days.

7. And finally, it's an official room for farts. Enough said.

Now go forth and bequeath a Man Cave. Your olfactory nerves will thank you.

Matt had long ago graduated from his miniscule spare bedroom in that first tiny rental house to an expansive den when we purchased our current home. And so, after taking a trip down memory lane to the inception of the Man Cave I decided it was fair, right, and just that I too have a space of my own.

After pondering mental images of libraries that resembled rooms in Hogwarts with soaring bookshelves and lead glass windows overlooking misty green valleys, I settled my feet back on solid ground and set about to transform the tiny white-walled third bedroom. I emptied it of unnecessary clutter, filling trash bags with notebooks left over from college, a dated lamp, and mounds of paperbacks with titles like *Flowers in the Attic* and *Daddy*. I got rid of the books because I had a sneaking suspicion my two favorite authors, J.K. Rowling and Eudora Welty, would never approve. Especially not Eudora. Southerners have enough stereotypes to fight without adding the brother-sister-romance-in-a-dusty-old-attic factor into the mix.

After the cleaning, I began to decorate. I angled the old lab table into the center of the room where I could see trees outside the window. I immediately did away with overhead lighting, placing lamps around the room and hanging a round paper shade in the corner. Matt found a wooden filing cabinet shoved to the curb in front of an empty house. Granted, it was painted black and plastered with orange-and-yellow 1970s wallpaper, but we lugged it home just the same.

We cleaned and painted it bright turquoise. A few weeks later I bought a set of metal baking shelves from a kitchen supply store, which served as sturdy bookshelves. A yellow vintage chair matted with layer upon layer of twenty-year-old cat hair was also scored from the curb, along with a cabinet and hutch painted the same shade of turquoise as the cabinet. It took me two days, two vacuum bags, and three lint rollers to clean the chair.

Vintage pottery served as pencil holders. Bowls of shells and beach rocks rested on the shelves, and an original Doris Day poster hung on the wall beside my desk. I hung bamboo blinds and white sheers and flung the windows open, smiling at my creation. I felt certain it was a room fit for an airy, wide-windowed farmhouse on Prince Edward Island.

It was as if having a designated space gave me permission to make writing a priority. I was working on a young adult book and not feeling particularly enthused about it, but the words of a former teacher kept ringing in my ears: "You have to write the bad stuff to get to the good."

And so I did. I kept writing. But there was one big obstacle in my way. The only unfinished decorating project in the office was a large blank wall behind my desk. It stayed that way for weeks. The longer it stayed blank, the less I wrote. I became convinced it was jinxing me.

I awoke one Saturday morning intent on finding something to remove the jinx, to fill that white wall behind my head. I donned a sweater, grabbed some coffee, and set off for a series of flea markets on the edge of town. I found dozens of dusty mirrors, vintage records, and travel posters, but nothing seemed right. After an hour of searching, my coffee and enthusiasm was gone. Defeated, I headed for the car. As I passed through the doorway, I glanced out of the corner of my eye and saw a series of frames stacked in a dark corner. I pulled them out one by one (doing my best not to shriek like a third-grade girl when a spider ran up my arm). There were old book prints and baptismal certificates, but at the very back of the stack were two matching white frames containing Jesus and Mary prints. I wiped the dirt from their heavy glass. They were very old.

"How much for these?" I asked an elderly man working the cash register.

He shrugged, "I don't know . . . twenty dollars?"

I didn't have the foggiest clue why I bought them. Surely Jane Austen didn't have Catholic art behind her head when she wrote. Maybe Flannery O'Connor, but not Jane. I didn't grow up in a house with religious art. The closest I'd ever come to it was in vacation Bible school, when the teachers re-enacted Moses and the burning bush with felt cutouts. Good Protestants, descendents of the Puritans, weren't supposed to need religious art.

I brought Jesus and Mary home, cleaned them off, and hung them on my wall. When I sat down at my computer, it felt peaceful with them behind me. I couldn't explain it, but as my mom later said, "I don't think you can go wrong writing with the Lord and Savior looking over your shoulder."

I liked being in their company, and yet, I was puzzled. When I entered my office and saw Jesus's face, I realized I had not spent much time thinking about him. I was reminded of my promise to Angela when I'd declared, "I'll pray for you."

One night I perched in my library, looking around with satisfaction. It was done. It was a cheerful room filled with books and pottery and the color turquoise. I examined the portraits behind my desk, eyeing a Savior I wasn't very familiar with. I watched him for a while and realized something important. As long as I didn't pray about the big things, I avoided being disappointed in God. If I didn't pray for Angela, and her cancer got worse, then I didn't have to be angry. But if I knelt before the face of Jesus in my office and prayed for her health and got a big fat *No* . . . what then? How did one process such a thing?

I knew full well how it got processed. If I prayed and she got sicker, I'd be miffed with Jesus. I'd be angry with God.

When you kneel before God and pray, you admit your helplessness. You admit that there's nothing you can do about a situation. And in praying, you admit that God is really up there. You concede He's really listening. And that, my friends, is no small revelation.

Truthfully, I was furious at the helpless feelings. Modern society is a "pull yourself up by your bootstraps" kind of place. We do and go and run and work and expect some element of control over our lives. Angela's diagnosis reminded me that sometimes we don't have control. Sometimes we are helpless. I didn't like that one bit.

Nevertheless, I'd promised her. I'd said, "I'll pray for you." I realized it was the very least I could do for her. I was reminded of her conversation with the homeless woman.

We were all sick in one way or another. We were all looking to get better, whether from cancer or poverty or the other bevy of daily problems that plagues us. Praying was the least I could do for someone I loved.

I looked up at the wall where Jesus hung and began. I wondered how clearly God could hear me. With all the other prayers and wars and sorrow in the world, how much did Elizabeth Owen's prayer count? Was it merely a whisper in the background of other more important requests?

But I prayed anyway. I prayed for perhaps the first time in my life, a prayer for something real and something important. And it felt good. The air in my library felt cleaner. My heart felt lighter. I was happy to have a room of my own.

CHAPTER 5

Sense and Square Footage

Marianne Dashwood had always dreamed of having a house full of children. On her first day as mistress of Norland Park she had decided the house would one day be full of laughter, baby carriages, and birthday parties.

Her new husband (dear, sweet Colonel Brandon) had managed to buy it back from her brother and his insufferable wife, making them an offer they couldn't refuse. One week later Marianne was back in possession of her ancestral home. Truthfully, she suspected Colonel Brandon loved the house more than anyone. He spent days prowling the mansion with a caulk gun and weather stripping, caring for the sprawling estate like a tender lover.

And now, after fifteen years of marriage and eight children, it was definitely full. One might assume that a manor as large as Norland Park would be able to hold scads of children comfortably between its historic walls. But Marianne was quickly discovering a major flaw in the house's layout, namely, its lack of adequate bedrooms. There were approximately five bedrooms, all of which were full and becoming fuller with the growing family of ten—number eleven on the way.

She cleared her throat and spoke up while dining on a breakfast of poached eggs and coffee. "Colonel Brandon, it's come to my attention that our family is bursting at the seams."

Colonel Brandon nodded distractedly, his head buried within the London paper. "Ummhhmmmm."

Marianne pursed her lips. "Ummmhmmmm" was a clear sign that not only had he not heard a word she'd uttered, but that he couldn't care less.

"Colonel Brandon!" Her voice was sharp as it echoed around the normally peaceful, sun-drenched dining room.

He frowned in confusion. "Hmm? What? Oh, I'm sorry my dear. What were you saying?"

"We. Need. More. Bedrooms."

"My dear, five bedrooms have been quite sufficient to hold generations comfortably for centuries," said Colonel Brandon.

Marianne shook her head. "The Dashwood family never had so many additions at one time dear, and we need to build more bedrooms."

"Perhaps we could just order more bunk beds?" Colonel Brandon offered, loath to tamper with the regal profile of Norland Park's original structure.

"Do you know what Jonathan did to William yesterday? He lodged a small horse carriage toy into William's left nostril."

Colonel Brandon frowned, disturbed to hear of such uncouth violence. "Well, I will certainly talk to him about that and—"

Marianne cut him off. "And do you know what Annabeth did early this morning?"

Colonel Brandon braced himself for impact.

"She stole the housekeeper's scissors and cut off a chunk of Margaret's bangs because, and I quote, 'Her dresses took up too much space in the closet.' You must accept facts. If we continue to buy bunk bed after bunk bed, we will soon be housing a brood of hardened criminals experienced in lock picking, hair cutting, and nostril stretching."

"There certainly must be another way," he mumbled.

"Well, we could always turn the blue salon into another bedroom for the girls, and wall off the breakfast nook for a nursery for the new baby."

Colonel Brandon nodded, his self-assurance evaporated and replaced by self-doubt and concern for his offspring's lack of self-control.

"But this can't go on forever," Marianne warned.

He sighed, "Fine, I'll consider building on a new wing."

"Good," Marianne nodded in satisfied approval. "Because this morning as I came downstairs, Vanessa informed me that Charlotte is refusing to wear deodorant. Then Vanessa wandered off, muttering something about straight razors and bald heads. Those girls need separate rooms as soon as possible."

Colonel Brandon stared bleakly into his cold cup of coffee. "All right. I'll meet with an architect tomorrow."

My alarm clock begins screaming at approximately six o'clock each morning. Usually, I'm able to manage mornings with a certain determination. After the initial "I'd rather walk on coals of fire than get out of bed" moment, I command myself upright and am comforted by the thought of a prework Starbucks run. I relish the thought of an unblemished day stretching before me with limitless possibilities.

But on one particular Monday, as rain hammered the roof and thunder boomed, my screaming alarm clock elicited a less than positive response. I hurled it onto the floor.

"Ugh! I don't want to go to work! I need a vacation! I need a shorter commute! I need coffee!" My personal list of grievances spewed forth and Matt groaned from his side of the bed.

"You'll feel better after a shower."

"I doubt it!" I sat up and gazed blearily out the window. The light outside was murky, a bluish greenish gray, and rain streaked down the glass in tiny rivers. "I'm having a hard time being happy lately."

"Why?" Matt's head was under a pillow, his voice muffled and sleepy.

"Because I don't have time to clean, or decorate, or write! I'm running around like a chicken with my head cut off."

I didn't really expect Matt to have a solution to my Monday morning funk, but it felt good to say it out loud.

"Liz, sometimes you just have to decide to be happy."

I blinked a few times, letting his words permeate my brain. And then I got mad.

"Decide indeed! That's the most clichéd phrase I've ever heard."

I jumped from bed and began getting ready as the storm raged outside. I stumbled around the house, slamming the coffee pot, pondering Matt's whole "decide to be happy" mantra. Maybe I'd just decide to be richer. Or skinnier. And while I was at it, I'd decide to take away Angela's cancer and make my husband more sensitive.

I patted Mabel's head goodbye and began rummaging in the coat closet for my polka-dot rain boots. I hunkered there, head beneath the coats, shoes flinging every which way as I searched, when lightning struck near our house. The flash and boom were instantaneous. The shoe rack crashed down on top of my head. Sandals and tennis shoes cascaded around me, burying me from the waist up. I stood up quickly, shaking myself free from shoelaces and flip-flops.

"You know what else doesn't make me happy?" I yelled, kicking the shoes out of my way. "The fact that our house has absolutely no closets! We need more space! It's just too small in here!"

I gave the door a satisfactory slam behind me and drove to work. I knew it wasn't Matt's fault I was in a foul mood. I knew it was an unreasonable way to spend a perfectly good Monday morning. But I couldn't help it. The day passed in a haze of filing and phone calls and suddenly it was noon. It was time for my lunch break, my time to visit Angela in the hospital.

A few days earlier the doctors picked up their scalpels and cut Fred the Undifferentiated Sarcoma out of Angela's arm. Her chemo schedule was on course and things were looking up.

"Think positively. And until your next scan, consider yourself cancer-free. It's the best way to approach healing," the doctor told her.

Bryan was at the hospital first thing every morning, and at night Angela's father Larry was an ever-present visitor. He brought little treats and magazines, along with his constant, quiet, comforting smile. But in the middle of the day I arrived so Bryan could get lunch or go home to check on the dogs. The middle of the day was my time to visit.

Angela's mother and sister were hundreds of miles away in another state, but they were planning a visit soon. Angela's face brightened at the mere mention of it.

The hospital room was quiet when I arrived. Rain pelted the large window facing the freeway and a fan buzzed in the corner. A nurse in the next room stated loudly, "Mr. Robinson, you gotta eat that piece of chicken. You need your strength. Let's try it again."

Angela greeted me with a wave.

"Come on, I know you threw up before, but let's just try this one more time," the nurse cooed.

"Foolish consistency is the hobgoblin of little minds," Angela quoted Emerson effortlessly, despite the dulling effects of pain medication.

It's hard to know how to behave while sitting with someone in the hospital. No matter how close your relationship is, the minute you shift it into the context of hospital wards and IVs and bedpans, things change. Where you used to lounge comfortably on the couch and make fun of bad movies, now one of you is lying in bed hooked up to machines, the other sitting in an uncomfortable chair and making conversation about the weather.

I myself am a doer. I want to run errands, bring food, read books, or clean something.

"Do you want me to bring you some more magazines?" I offered brightly.

"No, thank you," she motioned toward a stack in the corner that resembled the leaning tower of Pisa.

I frowned, scrambling for something else to offer. Angela clicked through the TV channels. I settled back in the chair and she finally paused on *Willie Wonka and the Chocolate Factory.*

"Do you know what I would prefer?" She turned to me and I sat upright, ready for my marching orders.

"Could you clear out some space in this room? I do loathe the feeling of a claustrophobic space, and frankly, this room gets tinier and tinier every time someone brings me something."

I glanced around the room, noticing for the first time how the plants, flowers, and floating balloons had taken over.

She pointed at a wobbling yellow smiley-face balloon floating in the corner. "And you can't imagine how scary that thing is when they give me extra doses of pain medication. It's just too small in here."

The room was tiny, and the flora and miscellaneous gestures of love from faraway family had indeed created the feel of a stifling greenhouse. I looked at the yellow balloon and began to laugh.

"What's so funny?" She sat upright.

"I had a total meltdown this morning. You know how I have to store my shoes in the coat closet? Well, the whole rack came crashing down on my head. And the last thing I yelled before leaving the house this morning? 'It's just too small in here.'"

Angela chuckled. "I'll take tiny closets any day. I feel like I'm in a jungle-themed shoebox."

Suddenly, the sound of whirring IV-cart wheels raced past Angela's doorway. The nurse from next door began to yell, "Mr. Robinson! Come back here!"

I jumped to my feet, noting a fleeing Mr. Robinson, his hospital gown flapping behind him as he stealthily maneuvered his IV pole through the hallway, his bare feet slapping against the linoleum floor.

"He's making a run for it!" I yelped.

Angela began to laugh loudly. "They probably put one of those yellow balloons in his room too!"

"Did I ever tell you what it was like growing up in a two-bedroom house with my sisters?"

Ang shook her head.

"What you said about living in a shoebox reminded me of it. We were a family of five living in a two-bedroom, one-bath house."

Angela smirked. "That sounds like the perfect storm."

"You have no idea. Every day I woke up to my parents yelling at each other, saying things like: '*Margaret!* I can't find my socks!'

"'They're in the cardboard shoebox under your bedside table.'

"'What happened to my drawer in the closet?'

"'I needed it for baby bibs and burping cloths.'

"'So where are my ties?'"

"'In the kitchen, in the drawer behind the dishtowels.'

"You should have seen all of us sharing one bathroom," I continued.

Angela nodded her head. "My sister and I shared a bathroom. She used to leave her Barbies in the bathtub and their plastic arms always impaled the bottom of my foot when I got in the shower. One morning I got so mad I took the whole lot of wet-haired mildewed dolls and threw them on her bed to wake her up."

She smiled at the memory, then settled back into bed and closed her eyes.

I grinned. The nostalgia of childhood sibling warfare is something that, eventually, becomes as sweet and comforting a tale as any romance or adventure.

It wasn't long after my eleventh birthday that Dad uprooted our family, sold our tiny bungalow, got a new job, and proceeded to make plans to build a home where he could store his ties and underwear without comingling them with kitchen utensils or running shoes.

In my father's Mr. Blandingsesque dreams, he pictured separate bedrooms for each of his daughters. No more scalped Barbies lying in the hallway, the unfortunate victims in our girlish turf wars over square footage. The fighting began with a chalk line down the center of the bedroom and ended with me clamping my hand firmly on Rebecca's forehead as she pressed her weight toward me, chomping her sharp baby teeth with ferocious fury, desperate to draw blood.

After two years of prepping, planning, cement pouring, dry wall dusting, and wallpapering, my father's castle was finished. Four bedrooms and three bathrooms were a beautiful omen of a peaceful domestic future for our family. We moved in, each girl gleefully running to her respective room with arms full of stuffed animals.

My room was bedecked in plush carpeting and Laura Ashley wallpaper. I scanned the walls, imagining where and how to hang my *X-Files* posters. My middle sister Rebecca raced to her room, quaint chair molding separating cornflower blue paint on the bottom and cheerful blue and yellow floral wallpaper on top. She flung herself into the center of the room and cried, "*Mine! All mine!*"

Rachel, the youngest at age three, wasn't quite as thrilled. Her emotions didn't scale the highest mountain; they remained skeptically within the valley of reserved judgment. As she scanned the confines of her pink bedroom at the top of a three-story, 3,000-square-foot house, she decided she didn't like it. In fact, she hated it. You see, Rachel was afraid of sleeping alone.

She tried to make it work. She trudged into her little pink-and-white bedroom every night, crawled into her big lonely bed, and gave it a shot. But somewhere around midnight, she always caved and crept into Rebecca's room.

Rebecca, on the other hand, was a mature six-year-old who relished her own bedroom and didn't appreciate these midnight visits. She refused to let Rachel in the bed. Many were the mornings we would find Rachel in Rebecca's bedroom, half standing, bent over the end of the bed, sound asleep. Rachel would rather sleep in a standing position for hours, like a cow in a field, than sleep by herself.

Of course looking back now, I find this heartbreaking. But as a thirteen-year-old who loathed her little sisters, I found the entire scenario hilarious. Every morning I looked through Rebecca's doorway to see Rachel (clad in polka-dot underwear and a hand me down T-shirt) slumped precariously, two feet on the floor, rump in the air, upper body beside Rebecca's feet. I'm not saying we took pictures. I'm not saying we didn't take pictures. All I'm saying is *if* there were pictures . . . even I have the common sense not to show them to the world.

I nicknamed Rachel "Sleeps Like a Cow."

Dad and Mom decided this could not go on.

Dad: "We built this house so these girls could have their own bedrooms . . . and by gosh . . . they're going to sleep in them!"

Mom: "I know. But we have to be gentle about how we approach this. She's still just a little girl. But I'm worried about her standing all night long; she could get a blood clot."

The women in our family have a longstanding history of paranoia when it comes to blood clots. To this day I refuse to wear knee-highs.

Dad: "Well, I'll get this straightened out tonight."

So nighttime came, along with a roaring storm. It was the worst possible timing. Dad tucked Rachel into her bed and picked up her favorite stuffed animal, Mr. Elephant. When times got rough, Dad always "talked" to us with our favorite toy.

"Rachel," Daddy bobbed Mr. Elephant's head as he spoke in a high-pitched voice, "I'm Mr. Elephant and I love you."

Rachel's face was stuck in a permanent scowl. She crossed her arms suspiciously.

"Now . . . you have this whole big bedroom that cost a lot of money."

The trauma of house-building expenses haunts Dad to this day.

Rachel slumped farther under the blankets, eyeing the storming blackness outside her window. She obviously didn't give a hill of beans about Dad's expenses.

Dad bobbed Mr. Elephant faster. "And I promise to stay here with you all night so you won't be scared."

Rachel's wily three-year-old eyes squinted into slits as she analyzed the situation. She knew full well that Mr. Elephant was not talking. She knew full well that once Daddy left and shut the door, she would be all alone in the dark and Mr. Elephant would be absolutely useless to her. She was not fooled.

"How about it Rachel? Will you be a big girl and sleep in your bed tonight?" Dad's optimistic voice bobbled in fake Mr. Elephant accent. Bless the man's heart. He was in completely over his head.

"*No!*" Rachel shrieked and jerked upright, reaching out and snatching Mr. Elephant from Dad's hands and hurtling him across the room. "I don't want to sleep with him! I want to sleep with something with *skin on it!*"

Dad's eyes widened. It was a tense moment. On one hand, Dad was sympathetic. It was stormy and she was only three. On the other hand, as he gazed into his youngest daughter's cherubic face, he was disconcerted at her use of the phrase "something with skin on it" to describe a living, breathing, human being.

Dad was faced with a decision. He could lose the fluffy talking animal act and order her to stay in her own bed. But he didn't have the heart.

"Well, um, just try to stay in your own bed, okay?"

Rachel eyed him, blinking a few times. Once he was gone and out of sight, she would wait for Rebecca to fall asleep and resume her sleeping place on the end of the bed. She knew it. He knew it. But like all good fathers, Dad knew when to cave.

I can't really remember when Rachel reconciled herself to sleeping alone. And after some time passed she came to love her own personal space. She came to appreciate Dad's hard work and the debt he accumulated all so she could have her own closet and a bathroom with double vanities.

I glanced at Angela. She was deep in slumber, the worry and pain wiped from her face. I realized that in the end, all of us, like Rachel, just want some company. I realized that Angela didn't need me to do anything. She didn't need another plant or magazine. She didn't need me to run errands or entertain her. When the dark storm sets in, when the surgeries happen, when people overload your claustrophobic hospital room with too many plants, when shoes avalanche from an over-crowded closet and whack you on the head, what really matters is the company of another beating heart, the presence of someone who cares about you, even if all they do is sit in a chair and bear witness to the trials at hand. In the end, we all, like Rachel, just want something with skin on it.

CHAPTER 6

Little Superwomen

The evening sky was a vivid lavender. Chartreuse trees towered over the lane to Orchard House. The spring air shimmered with cheerfulness as birds chirped and hopped about, fetching worms. But Jo March walked with a storm cloud above her head, trodding slowly, irritated by nature's bounty.

It had been a long day. A long, long, long day. A day that began with getting up too late to wash her hair or eat breakfast. A day spent hungry and afraid that her mild case of dandruff would become apparent to her grumpy employer, Aunt March.

Aunt March often went on tirades about women who didn't maintain "proper upkeep" of their appearances. But Jo wasn't stupid. She knew perfectly well Aunt March was alluding to Jo's disdain for acrylic nails and highlights, and the occasional forgetfulness that led to an upper lip in dire need of a Nair session.

Jo took a deep sigh and kicked a rock in front of her, accidentally flipping mud up onto her dress.

"Rats!" She wiped the mud haphazardly, smearing it across her best blue dress.

Jo paused in the road, gazing upward, pondering her life. Everyone around her seemed contented and prosperous.

Her friend Sally was married with two kids. Her schoolmate Martha was running her own seamstress business in a quaint whitewashed building downtown. Jo, on the other hand, was still living at home with her family, hadn't received a raise in three years, and couldn't remember the last time she'd shaved her legs, which were constantly chafing beneath her stockings.

Jo made her way up the front walk and unlatched the front door. She tossed her shoes and bag, rounded the corner to the front parlor, and threw herself on the floor in front of the fireplace.

"Ugh, this was the worst day," was all she could muster as a greeting to her family.

"Marmee's at the homeless shelter and asked if you would start dinner." Amy's shrill voice cut through the air like needles through an eyeball. Jo loved her youngest sister, but sometimes, in the darkness of night, she contemplated duct-taping her mouth shut.

"No. Meg can do it." Jo groaned, face down in the carpet.

"Well, someone certainly has their knickers in a twist," Meg huffed while working on her cross-stitching.

"You're darn right I do!" Jo sat upright, impassioned at the thought of working all day and being given a chore the moment she walked through the door. "I work full-time! I can't be expected to do laundry and make dinner and care about whether the bed is made! I cater to a crusty old woman for nine hours a day and her dog bit me the last time I tried to pet her. Plus . . . she farts!"

"The dog?"

"Aunt March! I'm exhausted. I don't care if we eat dinner or not. All I plan on doing tonight is sitting right here on the floor and if the spirit moves me, I might cry a little."

Meg swung her long dark locks over her shoulder, eyes flashing angrily. "I leave the house before dawn every day while the rest of you are sleeping! I'm exhausted too!"

Amy sat up straight, assuming as always that every argument and conversation revolved around her. "Well, I go to school all day with a professor that slaps me on the hand with sticks. My skin is so sallilitated . . . I cannot possibly prepare dinner!"

Jo rolled her eyes. "Sallila what? I've told you time and time again, stop making up words!"

"I'm not! Sallilitated means inflamed, red, and hurtful!" Amy stomped her little boot for emphasis.

"The proper word is irritated, you boob!" Jo heard her voice rise to a solid yell, but there wasn't anything she could do about it.

Beth coughed softly from her corner chair, where the cats were playing in her lap. "Just think of dear Marmee. She is always able to come home after a long day and smile with kind words for each of us. If Marmee can do it all, we should strive for perfection as well."

Jo rolled her eyes again, returning face down to the carpet. "You can't do it all, at least not without early crow's feet and a giant bottle of Xanax."

Beth smiled, "Just remember, birds in their little nests all agree . . ."

Jo groaned the groan of a thousand deaths and dragged herself off the carpet, marching toward the kitchen. "Whatever, Bethy. Birds in their little nests end up pecking each other to death, especially when they work full-time jobs. Especially when none of them have any more clean underwear for tomorrow. We're having sandwiches, by the way."

Louisa May Alcott modeled Marmee, the mother in *Little Women*, after her own mother, Abigail Alcott. She once wrote in her journal:

> *All the philosophy in our house is not in the study; a good deal is in the kitchen, where a fine old lady thinks high thoughts and kind deeds while she cooks and scrubs.*

I pondered this while driving to my parents' house one Friday evening. I was feeling less than perfect; these feelings of inadequacy usually swarm me once I'm captive behind the wheel, nowhere to walk, no way to distract myself. My normal drive-time talks with Angela would have helped, but she was on medical leave.

It had been a long week and as I arrived home Friday after work to find my husband facing a weekend at the office, I took one look at my filthy house and headed for the hills. Literally.

After being married several years, I had yet to achieve my ideal, *Little Women*–esque philosophy of living. I spent hours berating myself for being too exhausted after work to make sure we had clean towels. Each morning I raced out the door, dreading my bumper-to-bumper commute, forgetting to pay the bills until the cable company called during my lunch hour.

"Miss Owen, you owe us $68. Pay up or we'll cut off your husband's lifeline."

In short, I felt like a failure. As the lush green hills and cow fields flew by, I cranked up the radio, blasting Loretta Lynn and mentally reviewing the pile of shoes in our living room—the Owen household version of Stonehenge. I thought of the dust bunnies drifting beneath the furniture, little allergen-ridden menaces that formed in a matter of seconds after I swept the house. I thought about my daily morning rush to jump out of bed, slopping on concealer to mask the circles under my eyes, running a comb through my hair, and slapping a frozen lunch into a plastic bag before racing out the door looking like a harried *What Not to Wear* contestant waiting to happen.

I felt overwhelmed by life. Overwhelmed by the idea that womanhood and domesticity was a state of perfection, one that involved clean dishes, sweet smiles, and halos I would never wear. I was constantly looking over my shoulder, afraid someone would attack me with a needle and crimson thread. But instead of emblazoning an A on my shirt, they would embroider a capital L, for Loser.

I pressed the gas slightly, moving faster down the mountain highways as my thoughts returned to Louisa and all that "fine thoughts and kind deeds and cooking" stuff.

But here's the rub. No woman thinks "high thoughts" while scrubbing three-day-old macaroni and cheese in a baking dish. You know what she does? She curses under her breath, glances side to side to see if anyone is watching, and throws the whole mess into the trash can. And unless opening an overdue bill, gazing at your dirty, grease-splattered kitchen floor while wailing in frustration counts as "kind deeds," then Abigail and I were at a serious impasse.

Sure, Abigail might have preached high thoughts in the kitchen, but I guarantee at least once in her life she hurled a plate of crusted food across the room and yelled, "How many times do I have to ask you people to rinse your plate after you use it? What are you? Animals?"

I drove on, winding my way deeper into the Ozark Mountains, relieved to be putting my dirty house, hectic life, and foothills of dirty laundry behind me. I was on my way to spend time with my mother, a woman who didn't pander to preordained notions of womanhood. There were no unrealistic expectations in her house. Just art, Simon & Garfunkel records, and on occasion, nude oil paintings that still send me into fits of giggles.

I was on my way home, in part, because of Angela's orders. She had spent the previous evening listening to me bemoan my house's filthy condition and as far as I could tell, Angela did not suffer from my brand of housewife neurosis.

"So, do you have a cleaning schedule? How do you keep track of things?" I asked.

Angela chuckled, "I have a pretty simple to-do list. I make a grocery list, vacuum, and clean the bathrooms. Everything else can just bump along, in my opinion."

I stretched out on her couch and patted Sabi's head. Gerard tossed a ball in the air, trying to get my attention.

"I feel like Indiana Jones running from that giant boulder, you know? Like I'll never get ahead of all the work."

Angela nodded. "I used to feel that way. But time is far too precious to spend hours scrubbing grout lines or worrying that Martha Stewart might call you a loser. Dirt and I made a pact. I won't bother it if it doesn't bother me."

I bit my lip, suddenly embarrassed that I was talking about dust bunnies while my friend fought cancer. She shifted in her seat, wincing slightly. Her recovery from surgery was much slower and more painful than anyone had expected. She spied the look of shame on my face and laughed.

"Liz, don't look at me with such a morose expression. I'm alive. I plan on staying that way. And part of being alive is having friends who come over for tea and a healthy gripe fest about messy houses. I like it."

I smiled, thankful she had let me off the hook when she could have easily hurled a couch cushion at me while screaming, "You think you have problems? Wanna trade, you idiot?" After all, I would have deserved it.

"Just remember," she said as I rose to leave, "the universe doesn't care whether your kitchen is clean or not. You should get out of town, do something fun. Go see your parents."

I had to admit the idea was appealing. After all, I didn't feel the need to clean at my mother's house. There, in her universe, the dust bunnies didn't seem to bother me.

I relayed my frustration to my mother.

"Do you know what I did yesterday? I'll tell you. I worked eight hours, got stuck behind a wreck on the river bridge, got home an hour and a half later, threw sticks with Mabel and got a splinter, changed the sheets on the bed because they felt gritty, ate a bowl of cereal, balanced the checkbook, cried, weighed myself, cried again, and finally passed out on the couch. Of course my toilets are dirty! Of course we eat takeout! Of course my baseboards are dusty! How can I possibly be expected to do all this?"

Mother watched me placidly, paintbrush in hand. Slowly she began to shake her head. "Who cares? I raised my daughters to be creative and happy, not disinfecting, baseboard-washing experts. Come on, let's go to the fair. We'll watch the pig roping and I'll buy you a funnel cake."

I sniffed and nodded. This was a standard maneuver in our family, using food as a manipulation technique to cheer someone up or talk them off a ledge. But she was right. There was something tremendously soothing about the county fair, and I was always in the mood for a good pig roping.

While outsiders might visit our little county fair and find mountain people wearing manure-covered boots and licking ice cream cones (while yelling at their children "Eddie Joe, you poke your brother in the eye one more time and I'm gonna break off a stick and give you what-for with it") amusing and joke-worthy . . . I found it all homey and comforting.

We parked in a dusty lot just as night fell, the aroma of fried Twinkies filling the air around us, and I felt some of the tension falling from my shoulders. We paid at the gate, the distant cheering of the rodeo crowd and the carnival rides' pastel-hued lights distracting me from my dirty-baseboard-failure-as-a-woman conundrum.

We stopped in the first of three metal buildings, buying fresh-squeezed lemonade as my mother greeted some women from her quilting group. I smiled and excused myself, perusing the tables exhibiting raspberry jam winners, massive garden grown squash, bottles of red salsa, green pickles, purple beets, and homemade applesauce. Women milled about, greeting each other, sampling pies and admiring a giant pumpkin fit for Cinderella's coach. How did they do it? Did they work fifty-hour shifts and have enough energy left over to fertilize their gardens? Did they sew intricate wedding ring quilts on their lunch breaks?

After checking out the elementary art contest, my mom and I made our way to an outdoor pavilion to watch the Miss Stone County pageant. Next door, under a similar pavilion-like barn, the Stone County Livestock show was getting underway.

The swell of country music blasted from the cheap speakers as the sheep bleated in a nearby pen. The pageant contestants sallied forth onto a small stage, stepping awkwardly in stiletto heels, their skintight sequined dresses clinging to their hips and legs like neon tails from trailer park mermaids.

Smiling with the aid of Vaseline smeared on their front teeth, the girls walked the length of the stage, careful not to tilt their helmeted hairstyles. Their eyes were rimmed in black like surprised raccoons. These teens, who normally went to school in Ugg boots and skinny jeans, were preened, starched, sprayed, and zipped into disturbing versions of girl-women, their slightly wanting bosoms pinched and pushed upward by inserts in their strapless bras.

George Strait's voice crooned "Baby's Gotten Good at Goodbye" from the outdoor pavilion speakers, and the announcer read, "Amber likes to play basketball, solve math problems, and read books in her free time." I glanced sideways to the neighboring pavilion where handlers led their prized cows on a rope, parading them for the judges. Frankly, I was willing to go double or nothing that neither the cows in the livestock show nor Amber would ever be experts in higher-dimensional algebra.

"Why would they do this to themselves?" I said, my sense of feminist injustice thoroughly tweaked, although I didn't have much room to feel superior. The only reason my past wasn't besmirched with size 10 aquamarine formal dresses and rat's-nest hair was because my mother responded to my twelve-year-old request to "'do' pageants" with a solid, "Not in a million years. I'll set myself on fire first."

And then my stream of consciousness flowed straight toward the big river where all women eventually put their blame. Perhaps everything was my mother's fault? I thought of my own domestic imperfections, my dirty laundry, stressful job, and too-tight jeans. Perhaps if I had been allowed to participate in pageants, to plunk around in heels, and take home economics and sew boxer shorts out of happy frog-patterned fabric without my mother branding the project "a weird hat for Bugs Bunny," I would be farther down the road to domestic perfection. Perhaps, had I forged the trail of bouffant pageant hair and from-scratch chocolate cake recipes like the other girls, I'd be better equipped to deal with my job–house-quest-to-be-like-Martha-Stewart perfection issues.

I slumped in my chair, lulled into an odd Zen state by the low mooing of the nearby cow show and the *clomp clomp clomp* of the high heels on stage. I pondered my conundrum in its entirety. The girls began to parade out for round two, aka the Swimsuit Segment of the show. Nearby, a group of teenage boys began to yell, "Yeah yeah, git-r-mama, that's right, uh-huh girl," as the pitiful parade of glue-sprayed butt cheeks and Walmart swimsuits strode past us to the new tune of "Honky Tonk Badonkadonk" piped merrily from the crackling speakers overhead.

I wrinkled my nose. No matter how easy it might be to blame my current life crisis on The Margenator (a loving nickname my sisters and I gave to our mother, Margaret, after she single-handedly made the meanest teacher in school cry), it just wasn't so. Not only had Mom saved me from the cruel fate of the pageant circuit, she also strove to instill in her daughters a spirit of rebellion.

When faced with the question, "Every other girl in seventh grade is going to a party where they'll French kiss boys in the closet, why shouldn't I?" I could still hear my sage mother quipping, "Well, sure, it's the thing to do if you like herpes growing on your lips like the fungus eating the tree in the backyard."

And as I watched the girls return to the stage, back in their pageant garb, I smiled at my mom, patting her hand as she looked at me and said, "Can you believe this crap? Do you think any of these girls knows who John Singer Sargent is?"

Sure, Louisa's mom, Abigail, was probably one heck of a woman. And Louisa's literary creation, Marmee, was a beacon of motherly domesticity, her daughters a symbol of loving and harmonious womanhood. They had profanity-free vocabularies, starched dresses, prim manners, a tireless work ethic, and a lovely, clean, well-arranged home.

And that's why they call it fiction.

I studied my mother, a woman who had fought her whole life to give her daughters a sense of self-pride, a woman who had answered the religious question, "But why do women have to submit to their husbands?" with "Why in the world would you marry a man who would *want* a submissive wife?" And I realized that there is no such thing as womanly perfection. In the end, it doesn't matter if my baseboards are clean, laundry folded, bills paid, or my career climbing. The universe really doesn't care.

What matters is the warm feeling I get when I chill out, forget the stress, and spend an evening with my mother appreciating the absurdity of teenagers in drag-queen makeup parading next to prize-winning udders at a cattle show.

I bet Louisa and Abigail never had that much fun.

CHAPTER 7

Little House on a Shoestring Budget

Charles Ingalls's face glowed with excitement as he parked the wagon in front of his family's cabin.

"Caroline, come see what I brought from town!"

Caroline and the girls rushed from the cabin in great expectation.

Mary jumped up and down. "What is it, Pa? Did you buy some new calico for my dress?"

"Nope, something better." Pa smiled.

Laura clapped her hands, "Ooooh, I know! You brought some licorice!"

"No, guess again."

Caroline smiled sweetly and patted his arm. "Oh Charles, you shouldn't have. You bought those sewing supplies I wanted."

"Negatory." Pa swung into the back of the wagon and pulled a blanket from a huge box. "Just look at this, girls! Have you ever seen anything so wonderful?"

Caroline's brow creased. "But, Charles, what is it?"

"My dear, this is a brand-new, top of the line, home computer. It comes with a flat screen monitor, a wireless mouse, and lightning fast web capabilities. No more boring nights for us! After a long day of hard work we can prop up our feet and enjoy some real entertainment."

The girls stared blankly at the oversize box, nonplussed.

"But, Charles, that's a rather large purchase. Shouldn't we have discussed it? After all, money is awfully tight right now."

"Don't be a killjoy, Caroline. Money's made to spend, right?"

Caroline frowned. "I wouldn't spend that much money without planning first. And besides, I like playing cards and reading books at night. And what about your fiddling? The girls love it when you play music."

"Bah!" Charles shook his head, his high spirits refusing to be squelched by his wife's wet blanket attitude. "Live music and card games are a thing of the past. With this thing we can watch Hulu, get Facebook accounts, and e-mail your parents back east. We'll never be bored again!"

The next day Pa had the local cable company install Wi-Fi in the cabin and he crafted a new computer desk out of the finest oak. Laura and Mary quickly forgot their corn husk dolls as they became adept at uploading personal pictures for their Facebook accounts. Each night Pa insisted upon eating dinner in front of the computer so he could watch the local news as it streamed live.

Caroline did her best to be patient when she asked the girls to make the bed and was instead greeted with obstinate protests to go online and chat with boys from the next county. She took deep breaths and counted to ten when Mary showed her a blog called, "Cooking and Cleaning Tips for the Bored Housewife." But it was on a dark autumn night, with the fire crackling and Jack resting at her feet, that Caroline finally lost it.

"Charles." She put aside her knitting, crossing her arms sternly.

"Humph," he grunted, shoulders slumped in front of the mind-numbing blue glow of the computer screen.

Caroline glared at the back of his head. It had been four days since he'd showered, three days since he'd spoken, and two days since he'd changed his socks. This had to stop.

"Charles." Her voice was stern, carrying no hint of her usual serene demeanor. "I think it might be nice for us to have a family game night. We haven't spent much quality time together lately. Please turn the computer off."

"Not now, Caroline!" Charles snapped, two-day-old stubble shadowing his face. "I'm playing your mother on Wordtwist, and she's kicking my butt."

"That's it!" Caroline jumped to her feet. She marched across the room and yanked the computer cords from the wall.

"Hey!" Charles protested as the screen went black. "My score was up to one hundred!"

"I don't care!" Caroline basked in the shocked faces of her family. She knew she was normally the tempered, golden-haired domestic angel of the house. But ever since the new computer had taken center stage in the family room, she had seen herself become an irritated, overworked, ignored, electronics-hating madwoman.

"I don't care if we ever turn it back on! We're not made of money you know. I could have bought enough dress fabric for three years with the cash you spent on this computer.

And Charles, you've turned into a zombie. We haven't spoken more than ten words to each other all week. And girls, so help me if you don't stop posing and preening for your Facebook profile pictures, I'm going to throw that web cam down the well!"

Charles patted her arm sympathetically and motioned for Laura to bring his fiddle. "Would it help if we had a little music tonight?"

Caroline sniffled. "That would be nice."

"Great. Good. Music night it is."

Caroline smiled, relieved to see her husband blink more than once in a minute's time.

They gathered by the fire, and Jack nuzzled her hand to console her. Caroline sighed and hugged Laura's shoulders. She had her family back.

Charles opened his fiddle case and held up a hand cautiously. "We'll get started in just one minute. I just need to turn the computer on quickly, there's a website that has a new music arrangement for 'Oh! Susanna.' I'll just print it off..."

Caroline's mouth pinched into a thin line as the blue screen snapped back to life and the girls ventured to Charles's side. Slowly she reached down to pet Jack, who stared back at her in commiseration. They no longer lived in a simple little house on the prairie. They were now prisoners of the World Wide Web.

"Fine," Caroline spoke up, resignation replacing her righteous anger. "Hey, while you're at it, can you see if we can get

Mom and Dad on the web cam? I need to get Mom's recipe for banana bread before the potluck on Sunday. And move over Laura, I need to check our bank balance."

Once you have breathed in the deep pungent aroma of sewage, you never again forget the nose-hair singeing, eye clawing, throat clutching experience. It comes over you slowly. You begin to feel like a character in *One Flew Over the Cuckoo's Nest* as your muscles involuntarily jerk and you run around screaming and blowing raspberries. Anything to get away from the gag-inducing stench.

But let me explain.

It was 6:30 a.m. I was standing in my retro pink-tiled bathroom trying to open my bleary eyes and ready myself for work. As I stood there, peering into the mirror and wondering what demented nighttime fairy had planted four new wrinkles on my face, I paused and sniffed.

"Matt . . . what's that smell?"

Matt staggered from the bedroom in his underwear, eyes half shut. "I don't smell anything."

I pointed my nose into the air like a hunting dog. "Seriously? You can't smell that? Did you go to the bathroom in here earlier? I told you to use the room spray when you do things like that."

Matt puffed out his bare chest and gathered his pride as best a man can with sleep in his eyes and a small hole in the side of his underwear. "I just woke up!"

I frowned, catching a glimpse of my makeup-less hot-rollers-in-hair reflection and tried not to think about the fact that I looked fifty years old. "Well, help me figure this out. Because something smells ripe."

We sniffed the sink drain and ruled it out as a suspect.

"Is it coming from the toilet?" Matt asked, examining it from top to bottom.

"No, that's not it," I snapped. I'm not known for my milk of human kindness in a disaster. Don't get me wrong. I'm a survivor. I plan on eating my radish like Scarlett and clawing my way out of the nuclear dust while dragging my loved ones with me. But I won't be doing it with positive phrases and a smile.

"Hon, I just don't know. We'll call a plumber after work, maybe it's coming from under the house." Matt staggered a little, trying to get past me and out of our tiny bathroom.

"Well, that's just great." I moved aside and pulled the shower curtain back so I could lean on the side of the tub and give Matt room to move out the door.

That's when the full brunt of nastiness filled the air around us, a swirling mix of excrement and acrid stench that would have brought the sewer-dwelling Ninja Turtles to their knees. Where the normally slightly-clean-with-a-hint-of-soap-scum bottom of the tub should have been, there sloshed gallons and gallons of brown sewage.

I clutched the front of my sweatshirt and held my breath. Matt began to dry heave.

"Get out and shut the door!" I screamed as we bumbled into the hallway.

"I'll deal with this." Matt grabbed my shoulders, trying to talk and hold his breath at the same time.

I could feel my eyes glaze over, the horrors of typhoid and hepatitis in our bathtub filling my mind. But more importantly, I could envision our evaporated savings account. In my mind's eye I could see the long, gray hallway at the bank. A worker shrouded in a black suit pulling a set of keys from his pocket and unlatching a small locker labeled OWEN BANK ACCOUNT. Inside were two small stacks of quarters and a few crumpled dollar bills. It was bleak, not only because the banker with an unimaginative wardrobe gazed at me with an expression that could only be interpreted as "You're a Big Fat Loser," but also there was a very definite possibility we wouldn't be able to pay for a plumber.

I wasn't necessarily a spendthrift. In fact, I was downright frugal when it came to decorating with thrift store furniture and rewired vintage lamps. But the fact was, we were poor. We were starting out at starter jobs with starter salaries. We were starter adults with a starter bank account.

"Okay." I nodded numbly, thankful that Matt was taking the lead on such a disastrous biohazard. "But make sure the plumber is super cheap. We don't have much money!"

I left for work like a wino stumbling through a fog, not really remembering my commute, not really doing any work as I sipped my coffee and stared blankly at the computer screen. A disaster of such gargantuan proportions had previously been unthinkable in my life, and now I found myself attempting to push the image of a vast sea of bathtub poop from my mind. But I was sure of one thing: Anne Shirley never had to get ready for work while breathing raw sewage.

Angela leaned into the office doorway cheerfully. "Good morning."

"Morning," I grumbled.

She perched on the edge of my desk and adjusted her scarf. She'd been out on medical leave, and during that time she'd bought dozens of colorful scarves to wrap about her head and soldiered on as if nothing had happened. Bryan had started taking her to and from work since she was often too worn out to drive. And while I missed our commutes, I suspected they both enjoyed their car time together.

"What's eating you?" Angela quizzed.

"Nothing, I'm just tired."

Angela's green eyes narrowed. She took a sip of tea from a slender cat mug with a dainty handle and shook her head. "Tired my foot, what's wrong?"

I shrugged. "I'm not going to complain to you. It's not right."

"Pish posh." She waved her hand in the air. "So I had cancer. So I'm taking chemotherapy . . . so what? I want to be treated normally, which includes hearing my friend complain. Spill the beans."

"Fine." I sighed and took a sip of coffee. My mug was not dainty. It was double size and had a bright pink flamingo emblazoned across the front. "I have poop in my bathtub."

"Pardon me?" Angela paused, putting her mug down to give me her full attention.

"Ugh. I know. It's so gross, but our sewer lines are old and apparently they got backed up." I put my head in my hands.

"Well, you must take care of that immediately. You could easily contract something. Do you need to leave work? You just run out and I'll make excuses for you." A part of me really wanted to go curl up in bed and cry, but I didn't want to be at home with the stench.

I shook my head. "No, thanks. I appreciate it though."

"Well, the offer is on the table. Let me know what I can do," she said, turning and walking out the door.

I watched her leave, the navy blue scarf wrapped stylishly around her head, a pair of big gold hoops swinging cheerfully from her ears. I wondered how someone who was facing the biggest monster on Earth could be so cheerful, so upbeat.

The rest of the morning was a fog of filing and scheduling. At noon I went to lunch with my sisters. I didn't have time to mention my house disaster as Rebecca, my middle sister, leaned forward on both elbows and whispered secretively, "I've had the worst day."

Relieved to be comforted by someone else's life trials, I leaned forward as well. Our youngest sister Rachel, always the calmest and most rational of the three of us, remained uninterested.

"I had an eyelash disaster."

I frowned, immediately alarmed, "You ripped your eyelashes out again?"

Rebecca had, at the age of thirteen, survived a middle school basketball accident that culminated in the loss of all the eyelashes on her left eyelid. It was the most horrendous event in our family history, one which we had, to this day, been forbidden to speak of.

Rebecca tossed her mounds of yellow curls over her shoulder huffily.

"No. I lost my *fake* lashes."

"Of course you did," Rachel quipped, sipping her iced tea.

I leaned closer, trying to discern which set of mascara-caked lashes were deficient, but was unsuccessful. "What happened?"

"I don't know! There I was, sitting in a board meeting with our most important clients, and then—*bam*. The fake eyelashes on my left eye just fell off and plopped onto the table."

Rebecca was especially sensitive about her left eye, since it was the injured party involved in the basketball catastrophe, thus the reason for wearing a fake eyelash in the first place. It was her mission in life to warn perfect strangers in the Dillard's makeup department: "You treasure those eyelashes. Let me tell you from a personal trial of my own, those suckers just don't grow back very well."

"So," she continued, hands waving for emphasis, her Southern accent growing stronger to match her enthusiasm, "there I was, with the president and vice president, eyelashes on the table. I coughed and kind of just scooped them off the side and into my lap."

"What did you do then?" Rachel feigned interest, glancing toward the doorway of the kitchen to see if our food was on the way.

"Well, I clasped my hand over my left eye like this, and said, 'I just lost a contact.' Then I jumped up and left the room quickly, my eyelashes in my pocket. I ran back to my purse, grabbed my emergency eyelash glue, and slapped them back on."

Rachel elbowed me and smirked. "I'm fairly sure no one would have noticed."

"Of course someone would have noticed, Rachel! The whole situation was an absolute *chlamydia!*"

Silence settled over our table as Rachel set her tea glass down with a loud clink. I shook my head. "Wait, what are you talking about?"

"Oh, wait," Rebecca's eyes widened. "That's not the word I meant to use. I know it's a c-word . . ."

"Catastrophe?" I offered gently.

"Yes!" she snapped her fingers. "That's what I meant. It was an absolute *catastrophe!*"

Rachel, who had been up until this point the model of dignity and public manners, burst into a frenzied gale of laughter.

I started to laugh, but then it dawned on me that there was probably some version of chlamydia floating around in my bathtub at that very moment.

Rebecca leaned forward, hissing, "Shut up, Rachel! You have no idea the feeling of imbalance and vertigo one gets from having an uneven set of eyelashes. It actually affected the way I walked."

"Excuse me?" Rachel was crying now, imagining our big-haired sister, staggering in high heels to her cubicle, blinking spastically, desperate for rebalanced eyeballs.

"Well, it did!" Rebecca insisted, banging the table for emphasis. "I could feel the heavy lashes on my right eye, and the bareness of my left. Anyway, one good thing that's come out of this, I'll spring for the expensive lashes next time. It just doesn't make sense to cut corners when it comes to something as important as good eye makeup products."

I smiled, doing my best not to join in Rachel's horse laughter. I would save that for later in the car. But as I made my way back to work I felt better about the sewage in the bathtub. I always felt better about my life after remembering Rebecca's seventh grade eyelash debacle. Most life disasters—such as my bathroom catastrophe—could be set right again, but her eyelashes were gone forever.

The day flew by, Matt called to tell me the plumbers were on their way to the house and, even more importantly, the overall cost would be far cheaper than we'd thought.

"It's $120. We can swing that right?"

I sighed. "Just barely, but yes, it should be fine."

The rest of the day was productive, positive, and a complete 180 from my morning. As Angela and I walked to the parking lot after work, she patted me on the shoulder.

"Let me know if you need help. I'll bring my cleaning gloves and come straight away."

I gawked at her, trying to take the breadth and generosity of her statement in. Then I grabbed her and hugged her. I could barely get Matt to pick his underwear up off the floor. Never in my wildest dreams did I imagine anyone volunteering to help me clean crap in a bathtub.

Angela stood stiffly and then patted my shoulder again brusquely. It wasn't that she minded being hugged; hugging just wasn't her go-to form of expression. I knew that I would never ask her to help me clean up feces. I also knew I'd never forget her offer to help.

When I arrived home, the plumbing van was in the driveway, emblazoned with big red lettering, BARGAIN PLUMBERS. Matt was home, and I could hear men in the back of the house working and talking to each other.

Matt met me at the door. "It's just a clog. They said they see this all the time with old houses and it's no big deal."

"Awesome." I gave Matt a hug and we stood, clasping hands and smiling at each other until an Earth-shattering sound filled the air. Mabel, who had been standing at our feet wagging her tail, bolted for her hidey-hole under the dining room table.

The horrendous sound was reminiscent of thousands of shattered pottery pieces. We raced to the hallway and through the bathroom door. Where once our toilet had been was now a gigantic whirling piece of black metal, bursting through our shattered toilet and spinning around the bathroom.

It's amazing the clarity of mind that takes place during a home repair disaster. Instead of screaming and tearing out my hair, I stood there, transfixed, thinking to myself, "Huh. Well whaddya know? It's like a plumbing and sewage version of *Anaconda*."

The monstrous plumber snake destroyed everything in its wake. It flung sewage and brown horror everywhere, catching the bathroom curtains in its spin, ripping them from the window. The fabric twisted around the metal snake into an unrecognizable wad, spattered and brown.

Somewhere in the backyard a man began to yell. There was more shouting about "pipes not up to code" and "sometimes this happens" as Matt watched in horror at the weapon of mass destruction wreaking havoc in our bathroom. He began to shout, *"You're going to replace this toilet or I'm going to come over and use your front yard as my own personal bathroom!"*

And then the snake retreated back down into the ground from whence it came, leaving a shattered toilet, flooded floor, and poop-splattered pink tiles in its wake.

This is also the reason, incidentally, that I now avoid the color combo of pink and brown at all costs, especially in a bathroom setting.

"Well," Matt spoke slowly. "I guess this is what happens when you use a company called 'Bargain Plumbers.'"

I sized up our bathroom, pondering the Hazmat suits and gallons of bleach that we would need to set everything right again.

I continued to stand there as the plumbers came inside and examined the broken toilet, promising to fix and clean everything. And as I stood gaping at the war zone previously referred to as "the powder room," I remembered Rebecca's cheap eyelashes.

Bargain shopping had left her at the mercy of uneven eyelashes, embarrassment, and vertigo.

Bargain shopping had left us with a bathroom that had legitimately earned the right to forevermore be referred to as "The Crapper."

Either way, whether it comes to cheap synthetic lashes plopped onto a boardroom table, or a whirling plumber's snake leveling your toilet, sometimes it makes sense to pay more.

But paying for the best takes money. Dough. Moolah. And so I began to dwell on our financial status. I found myself glaring at people who drove BMWs or shopped at specialty food stores. I was poor, and I didn't like it.

In the days that followed I began to haunt money-saving websites. I sought out books written by economic gurus. I was determined to find a way out of our paycheck–to-paycheck life.

Angela took notice of my obsession with quiet patience. One afternoon we ate lunch on a park bench as I climbed onto my soapbox and she listened.

"I mean, when you think about the amount of money we spend on things that aren't even necessities, it flabbergasts me. For example, toilet paper prices are outrageous. We spend hundreds of dollars a year just because the word 'plush' is on the front of the packaging. Pioneers didn't even have toilet paper. They used leaves. Leaves are free."

Angela pondered my statement seriously, the shadow of a smile lurking on her face. "That's true. Leaves are free, but not very sanitary. I guarantee the pioneers had frequent rashes and interesting body aromas."

I felt my face flush with shame as I looked at her. She was bald, her skin was pale, and her eyelashes were gone. To add insult to injury, her latest scan revealed a cancerous lesion on her lung. It meant another surgery, another hospital stay, and an even slower road to recovery.

The doctors had comforted her.

"When we do the next surgery, as long as the margins are clear, you should still consider yourself cancer-free."

"I think perhaps they're yanking my chain," Angela had noted.

I found myself staring at the ground, ashamed of my leaf versus toilet paper rants.

"Listen, I'm sorry. You're battling the toughest thing on Earth and here I'm telling you about my prejudices against plush toilet paper."

She chuckled, "Do you think I want to sit around and talk about cancer? I just want to feel like me, not a science experiment that doctors poke and prod. So actually yes, I adore hearing about your toilet paper expenses. When Bryan and

I were first married, we had a roommate to help with rent. You do what you have to do to get by. But you're being too hard on yourself. You and Matt are doing the best you can, and that's good enough. And if I come over to find a basket of leaves in your bathroom, I'm taking you to a therapist."

I knew Angela was right. I even smiled and laughed. I was grateful I hadn't offended her with my insensitive talk of toilet paper in the face of her life-threatening illness. But despite her logic and good humor, I couldn't stifle my inner urge to hoard money like a dog burying bones or a raccoon filling its nest with shiny objects. I was a woman on a mission.

A week later, I had an epiphany.

We were on our customary nightly stroll, a form of entertainment long held sacred by poor people. And we were definitely poor.

"It's really hot tonight," Matt commented as he reached out and squeezed my hand.

"You can say that again. Can you ever remember a heat wave like this in late fall? It feels like July. My right armpit is practically gushing with sweat. Why do you think that is? I sweat only in one armpit and not the other. Mom used to worry that I had a gland problem but . . ."

I trailed off as I noticed Matt's sideways glance. It was clear what he was thinking. He was pondering how years earlier he had married a sweet, adorable bride, and now he found himself attached for all eternity to a woman who liked to ponder the uneven distribution of sweat in her pits.

I put the kibosh on the armpit talk and struggled for a way to change the topic. I was trying to reclaim a tiny bit of allure, but all I got out was, "Hey, let's watch a movie when we get home."

That's something else poor people do. They watch movies at home, because that, too, is free.

Matt nodded enthusiastically and we turned back in the direction of our house.

I pondered our diminished financial state. There was supposed to be a pot of gold at the end of the rainbow known as college graduation, and I was determined to find it.

"We need a bigger savings account," I stated.

"How do you define bigger?" Matt asked.

"Well, really any amount over $75 would be an improvement."

"Eh, cut us some slack. We have huge student loan payments. We just bought a house. Things will get better." Matt smiled the smile of an eternal optimist. I was instantly irritated.

"Things don't just get better on their own you know," I chided. "We've got to really tighten our belts. We need to sock away every single cent we can, that way I won't have to have a nervous breakdown every time the bathtub fills up with six months worth of sewage."

Matt kissed the top of my head. "I doubt that will be a recurring event, but whatever makes you happy."

I smiled back, happy to have the green light on a new plan. I knew what would make me happy: cold, hard cash.

Suddenly I was reminded of second grade and my class's six-week study of the Little House books by Laura Ingalls Wilder. We read aloud about the wolves in the north woods. We churned butter on the blacktop. We contributed to a giant bulletin board that stretched the length of our classroom wall and depicted Laura and her family, their domestic cabin, deer in the woods, pine trees, and a sunset.

Laura's "little house" shaped my childhood ideas of domesticity. I believed that true homemaking consisted of baking fresh bread over a fire, stacking logs to make a house, and Pa carving a fireplace mantle etched with stars and moons. Can't afford a house? No problem, just dig one underground near a flowing stream. Budget too tight for groceries? Again, no problem. Just hunt quail.

But as I was learning, the modern world had no room for "little houses," a winter's worth of venison, or a hand-carved fireplace mantle, mostly because they are all against building code and hunting regulations within city limits.

I pondered these things as Matt once again squeezed my hand and we waited by a red light to cross a street. I watched the cars zoom by, turning in and out of the nearby strip mall. I thought of my own poverty and was wistfully reminded of the Ingalls family and their simple covered wagon. I thought of Ma's frugal ways, Laura and Mary's wooden dolls, a Santa Claus that forged swollen streams with nothing but determination and a team of mules. It all seemed so far away from the modern world, a world of walk-in closets specifically built for shoes and a set of dishes for every occasion.

Why must we have all these things? Why couldn't we be content with the simple things in life like the Ingalls family? That night I set my resolve. We too would model our lifestyle after our pioneer ancestors. We'd be rich in no time.

By the time we got home I felt much better. And so, my mission began. I would embrace frugality. I would grow tomato plants and cool myself with a homemade fan made of cardboard. If Laura could do it, so could I. We didn't need the trappings of the materialist modern man. We just needed a savings account.

I began to keep a journal of our simple life quest.

Day One: Cooked beans and ham in a slow cooker. It will feed us for the entire week. Laura would be proud. Unfortunately, we now need to buy Beano.

Day Two: Turned off the air conditioner and hung a bag of ice in front of small electric fan. It seems we're having an Indian Summer. I'm sweating and have a mild case of vertigo, but other than that we're in fine shape. Late day update: Matt threatened to move in with my grandmother across town.

Day Three: Got invited to a Mary Kay party and declined, telling my friend, "Makeup is wasteful, I don't wear it anymore." Later Matt examined my face in alarm, asking me if I was coming down with the flu. I immediately purchased concealer and mascara at the Dollar Store.

Day Four: I suggested that we cut off cable and use the extra money to buy a bread maker and a sewing machine. Matt immediately called my grandmother and asked her how much she charges for rent.

Day Five: I decided to go to the grocery store on foot. After walking eight miles in the noonday heat, I stopped at Sonic, bought a Cherry Limeade, and hitched a ride from a woman named Rhonda.

Day Six: DVD player broke. I suggested we read aloud to each other by candlelight. Matt shed one small tear.

Matt was truly devastated by the loss of his beloved DVD player. It was, after all, his one source of entertainment, a great shining escape from days spent designing ads and pacifying clients' demands. So it was with great amazement and trepidation that I watched Matt set his jaw, roll up his sleeves, pull out his tool set, and proceed to take the plastic top off the defunct DVD player.

As I gazed at him, I was reminded of my Little House ideals. While I didn't necessarily feel the DVD player was a must with regards to our financial future, I couldn't help but admire Matt for setting out to deal with the situation in a frugal manner. Nevertheless, I found the process worrisome.

"What are you doing?"

"It won't eject a DVD. It's stuck in there. I'm going to fix it," Matt said, eyeing a barrage of circuits and computer chips, a small screwdriver in his hand.

I eyed the tiny green and red wiring and circuit boards. Then I made a rookie mistake. I challenged his manhood.

"No offense, but . . ."

(It should be noted that at no time during a marriage, any marriage, should a sentence begin this way.)

". . . I don't think this is a good idea."

Matt glanced at me briefly. "Why?"

"You don't know what you're doing! Besides, this is just another trapping of our materialistic society. We have all kinds of free entertainment. I have tons of books, there is the local library, and we can take more walks . . ." I trailed off as Matt gave me an icy stare.

I shifted from one foot to another, realizing the inevitability of Matt's foray into the unknown world of electronic repair. My stomach knotted. "Fine. Maybe we should have someone else fix it."

Matt paused and made a face I now refer to as The Wounded Animal. He stopped blinking, shifted his lower jaw slightly to the left and raised his eyebrows.

"Just what are you trying to say?"

I realized my faux pas. It suddenly dawned on me that he thought that I thought he was stupid. I was supposed to smile sweetly and unquestioningly rely on him to fix everything from flat tires to, apparently, complicated modern electronics for which he had never been trained nor read an instruction manual.

Now, we all know our husbands are flawed. We all know that they howl and complain about how much a licensed handyman charges for plumbing services as they pull out a set of tools and proceed to flood our kitchen floors with water from under the sink. But what a seasoned married woman knows is the secret to finessing the situation.

For example, the seasoned married woman says: "Sure, honey, I know that it's much cheaper if you install the sprinkler system in our yard. But don't forget my car needs an oil change. Why don't you take care of that and we'll just hire someone to install the sprinklers. After all, you work so hard to take care of me, and I don't want you to be overly stressed."

See? True finesse. Utter genius.

On the other hand, the naïve married woman says: "Are you kidding? Install a sprinkler system? You must be joking. Remember the time you installed our first deck? And it sloped at a forty-five-degree angle and the grill kept sliding off the end? Remember how the neighbors called it The Leaning Deck of Bill? Forget it, I'd rather pay money and hire someone to do it right."

Needless to say, at this particular juncture, I was the naïve married woman.

"Well, all I'm trying to say is, we should let a professional do this. You're just making me nervous."

"Thanks a lot for thinking I'm dumb." Matt sniffed and returned his attention to the DVD player.

I tried to distract myself. I really did. Instead of watching over his shoulder like an anal algebra teacher, I eyed the fluorescent light fixture above and dreamed of a wrought-iron chandelier with candles, one like Laura might have had in her farmhouse. I counted the number of wood planks from one side of the floor to the other, wondering what it would be like to have a dirt floor. But even that didn't work.

"Seriously," I couldn't stop myself, "let's just not worry about this. We don't even need to watch TV."

Matt stood up, smiling smugly. "Speak for yourself. And besides, it should work now."

"Why? What did you do?"

"I'm not sure, but I moved some wires around. I feel good about it."

I felt my mouth hang open as visions of exploding electronic equipment burying itself into the drywall filled my head.

I tried my best to hide the skepticism and distrust splashed across my face. The last time we had a flat tire his solution had been to pump it full of fix-a-flat, drive very fast, and say, "There, that should hold it for another few months." It only stood to reason that if he couldn't replace a tire properly, our DVD player didn't stand a snowball's chance in hell.

"Now," he paused and reached for the cord, "let's just plug it in and see."

With the top of the DVD player still bare, wires exposed, he plugged the cord into the electrical socket and pushed the eject button. We listened to a buzzing sound inside the guts of the player, but nothing happened.

"*Dangit!*"

Except Matt didn't say dangit.

I felt an ominous foreboding about the entire situation, but I was quite certain that in Laura's blissfully simple life she'd never had this argument with Almanzo.

"Let's just leave it alone, really."

"This should have worked!" Matt gritted his teeth. "I'm going to try one more thing."

"Fine." I whirled and walked out of the room. "But I still say we don't need that thing to be happy. People lived perfectly contented existences before anyone invented TVs or DVD players!"

I slumped on the couch, flipping through a book, determined to ignore the goings-on in the kitchen. And then, Matt screamed.

It wasn't a regular scream. It was the kind of scream a calf makes when a rancher sears the flesh on its backside with a red hot poker.

I threw my book across the room and whirled around the corner to the kitchen. There was Matt, all six-foot-one of his massive frame, curled into a tiny kitten-like ball on the kitchen floor. The small screwdriver rolled beside him, the DVD player still plugged in.

"Matt!" I shrieked, crossing the room in two long strides. I knelt down, cradling his head in my lap. His eyes wobbled like unstable marbles, but an odd smile appeared on his face.

"You tried to work on it while it was *plugged in?* You could have been electrocuted!"

Matt's eyes finally came into focus, the odd smile still in place. "Yes . . . but I fixed it. Look."

His unsteady hand pointed up at the DVD player on the counter. Sure enough, it had spit out the jammed DVD and was ready to play. I breathed a deep sigh, staring back down at my husband who had been willing to risk life and limb to repair something I had deemed financially frivolous.

"I know you can save money by reading books and playing cards and taking walks," Matt looked up at me with pure joy splashed across his face, "but I can't. I need TV. I need movies. I need them. I'll get a second job if I have to."

I felt my thrifty, Grinch heart begin to thaw as I examined my electro-shocked but happy husband, a man willing to face the fate of convicted death row inmates to reclaim his place in the modern world. Perhaps I had been mistaken. Perhaps a bathtub full of fecal matter had tripped the circuit breaker in my brain and caused a major blackout of logic and reason.

"Okay. Maybe I've been going a little overboard." I pushed the hair from his forehead.

"So can we stop washing our plastic sandwich bags?" Matt's eyes were pleading.

"But that really saves a lot of money!" I protested.

"Okay, but will you stop hitching rides to the grocery store? It's dangerous. I don't care if Rhonda was listening to a Glenn Miller CD in her car."

"Yeah," I said.

"And Liz . . ." Matt's eyes were pleading. "I guarantee if the Ingalls family had had a choice, they would have loved air-conditioning. Can we please turn it back on?"

I sighed as I helped him off the floor and unplugged the DVD player. "Yeah, I'm cool with that. Actually, I've been pretty worried that I'll ruin most of my good shirts. The sweat in my right armpit is pouring like a rainspout . . ."

CHAPTER 8

Wherefore Art Thou, Pest Control?

Soft yellow light flickered from the candelabras. The banquet table was spread with crimson roses and Mrs. Capulet's best china. The servants scurried in their finest black-and-white uniforms as they carried platters of olives, cheese, and wine glasses.

"Juliet!" Mrs. Capulet's piercing voice rattled the nearby dishes as she leaned around the corner to look up the staircase. "Hurry up and help me! The guests will be here any minute!"

Juliet appeared from her room, her long shiny locks pinned in romantic curls, her shoulders slumped in a sign of teenage disapproval. She would have rather covered herself in honey and rolled around on an ant hill than attend one of her mother's parties.

"Would it kill you to smile?" Mrs. Capulet smoothed her graying hair and pointed a finger. "I won't have you mooning around over that Romeo bum forever. Your father's boss is coming tonight and some other very important guests, so try to show a little enthusiasm."

Juliet crossed her arms. "But Mother, he's not a bum. If you took the time to get to know him . . ."

Mrs. Capulet let out a huffy laugh. "Please. All those Montagues are the same. Accountants, paper pushers, middle management. What you need is someone who climbs ladders, like your father."

Before Juliet could roll her eyes, the doorbell chimed and her father's boss swept through the arched doorways. Mr. Smith was escorting his third wife Vanessa, who at one time had been a cocktail waitress with magenta hair and a nose ring. But no one mentioned that now.

Mr. Capulet emerged from his library, his booming voice filling the room. "Welcome! Celia, honey, take our guests' coats and for heaven's sake, let's all have a drink before I pass out."

Juliet gagged a little. This picture-perfect postcard dinner party was a sham. A sharp poke in the eye. A silk hat on a pig. While the silver might be polished to a high shine and the house decorated within an inch of its life, she knew full well it was a carefully crafted facade.

Despite their position and money, Mr. Capulet still belched and scratched himself while watching NASCAR. Mrs. Capulet, despite numerous surgeries, still looked like Gollum underneath all those layers of makeup. And on very rare occasions, she would forget her fake airs and yell at her children, "You'uns better wash your hands before I whoop every one of ya!" And then Mr. Capulet would cackle, "Celia, your redneck is showing."

"Juliet," her mother's face was pinched, her smile hindered by Botox. "Will you please make sure everything in the kitchen is ready?"

The doorbell rang as Juliet turned to leave and a few more guests filed through the door. She gave a deep sigh and began making her way across the foyer when something strange happened.

"What is that?" A woman shrieked as a black object began to zigzag across the marble floors and through the crowd.

And that's when Vanessa reverted to her cocktail waitressing roots as she cursed and then screamed.

"Roooooach!!!!"

Horror and panic struck the crowd as they scrambled away from the half-dollar–size bug, its wings outstretched, threatening flight.

Juliet was conflicted, torn between laughing hysterically as women tried to climb onto their husbands' backs, and horror as the little black roach made a beeline for her.

She didn't have time to react, because the little-roach-that-could took flight, streaking toward her like a disease-filled missile, zooming right under the hem of her dress and clawing its way toward the elastic at the bottom of her undergarmets.

Panic overtook her as she felt the roach's little claw-like legs skittering up her bare leg.

"Get it out!" She started to shriek and stomp her feet, hoping to dislodge the bug that remained steadfast in its upward climb toward her nether regions.

The faces of those around her blanched, horrified as it dawned on each of them what was happening. Her father made a mad dash across the room, helpless to do anything.

Juliet thought she might faint as she tried to decide which was worse: taking her clothes off in front of all her father's coworkers before the roach reached her underwear, or existing for one more moment with a scabby, needle legged bug clawing its way up her leg.

Vanessa continued to curse in sympathy of her plight as Juliet, in desperation, lifted her skirts high over her head.

"Juliet! Remember yourself!" Mrs. Capulet shrieked.

But it was too late, her skirts were lifted and undergarmets were exposed to all the dinner guests.

With one hand, she reached down, grabbed the section of cloth where the roach was scurrying, and crunched the little bug as hard as she could. The cracked walnut sound filled the room and Juliet tried not to gag as she realized she'd just killed a bug with her bare hands, inside her own undergarments.

"Oh heavens!" Mrs. Capulet swooned, falling into Mr. Smith's arms. Most of the guests looked ill, but Juliet thought she spied a look of respect and approval from Vanessa.

Ask any homeowner in insect country if they have a pest contract and they'll bug their eyes (no pun intended) and nod.

"Heck yes, I do! Best money I ever spent!"

I am no exception.

The weather outside had turned cold. The floors were cold. My nose was cold. The wind rattled the windows and Matt was working late again. Rebecca came over and we settled in the den to watch a movie.

"You want popcorn?"

"Yeah, but I want my own bowl."

I reached into my china hutch for the perfect size bowls, when movement in the corner of my eye caught my attention.

A black roach, wings outstretched, scurried across the floor of the breakfast nook.

I hear you. I know what you're saying.

But Liz, every house has bugs.

Not like this they don't.

"*Roach!*" I screamed, hurling my shoe across the room. I missed him as he disappeared into the den.

I raced around the corner, scanning the floor.

"Did you see that? Did you see the roach?"

Rebecca stared at me, undisturbed beneath her cozy quilt, her legs propped up near the crackling fireplace.

"Just calm down."

Rebecca was the designated bug-battler in our family. Even as a child she would charge into my bedroom and whack bugs with her shoe while I screamed in high-pitched thirteen-year-old tones. Nothing had changed. She still killed bugs for me. I, on the other hand, still squealed like a thirteen-year-old girl.

"It was huge, and its wings were all spread out and threatening! I'm pretty sure it was angry."

"Roaches don't have human emotions, but they do hiss for protection. Their blood is white, and a female usually gets pregnant only once and stays that way for almost her whole life."

I glared at my sister, the keeper of all Discovery Channel knowledge, when all at once the roach in question made its presence known. It appeared from under the couch, wings outstretched like a bat. It made lift-off in one smooth motion, zooming into the air, eye-level with Rebecca. She swung her arms in self-defense, but it was too late. Mr. Roach embedded his body into her hair.

I screamed. She screamed. Mabel hid under the table.

Rebecca began to slap her mounds of blonde curls. "It hurts! It's scratching me!"

I watched helplessly. Let's face it, bugs scare me to death. Even if there was something I could have done, I probably wouldn't have.

She began to gag, still slapping her head. "Oh my stars, I think it just farted on me! It did! It farted on me!"

The roach, tired of being pummeled, popped out of Rebecca's hair and fell to the floor with a smack. She picked up a coffee table book and slammed it down, smashing him with a decidedly fierce squishing sound.

She continued to gag. "My hair *reeks*. It really did fart on me!"

Great. Like I needed one more reason to be terrified.

"Bugs don't fart, do they?"

After Rebecca washed her hair with Dawn detergent, we looked it up on Wikipedia. Not only do cockroaches fart, they do so every fifteen minutes.

Little did I know it at the time, but that night was a harbinger of the infestation to come. I suppose the notorious farting roach was hiding underneath the house or the water heater closet, safe from the chill outside. Or rather, it was probably Mrs. Roach, because someone, somewhere, laid eggs.

While Matt has always been stricken with terror over spiders, I am most horrified by cockroaches. And now these little monsters had taken up residence in my spice cabinet, pooping and proliferating at frightening speeds. We set off bombs, we sprayed, and each day they gained momentum, setting up an alien colony right under our noses. They also grew bolder, scooting beneath our feet like tiny kamikazes and carrying out daring raids of the pantry every night.

As time passed I began to believe that the cockroaches infesting our home were a new breed, a superhuman breed. Had other people encountered such a scourge? If they had, surely the nightly news would be peppered with stories of homeowners gone mad, setting their homes ablaze and dancing naked in the front yard while singing "ding dong the roach is dead" before being confined to an institution for the rest of their lives.

And so we called the local pest control company. They came, they extinguished, and they placed third in my list of heroes behind Dolly Parton and Ramona Quimby. The cockroaches were dead.

Matt, on the other hand, did not make out as well as I did. Apparently, his arch nemesis, Mr. Spider, was not so easily killed by the bug man's sprays and fumes.

Matt is a big man: barrel-chested, a former football player, and an all-around imposing fellow. Until he sees a spider.

I was enlightened with this knowledge early on. On our second date he dropped me off in front of my college dormitory, leaned in to kiss me, and gasped, suddenly jerking upright and slapping his knees with the fury and speed of an addict on methamphetamines. It was dark, but thanks to the streetlight outside, I caught the silhouette of a tiny spider, legs flailing, as it flew from Matt's lap right toward my feet. I proceeded to shriek and stomp wildly. Moments later I realized that Matt had not only flung the spider on me, but jumped from the cab of the truck and slammed the door, leaving me to do battle alone.

There was no goodnight kiss that night.

A month after pest control vanquished the terrible, farting cockroaches, we had another freakish ordeal. I unlatched the dishwasher to find a rather large, soggy, dead spider lying on the door.

"Ew!" I exclaimed. "It must have gotten trapped inside and drowned."

Matt took a deep breath, puffed out his chest bravely and stepped forward. "Wait. I need to do this. I'll get this one."

My eyes widened in admiration as he gripped seventeen paper towels, closed his eyes, and plucked the waterlogged spider carcass from the dishwasher.

"Wow, baby, I'm impressed."

He grinned at me sheepishly, much like a surgeon who had just made his first incision or a pilot after flying his first successful mission. But when he cast his eyes toward the paper towels, the smile faded. His flesh blanched white, his pupils dilated.

"It's. Coming. *Ouuuuuuuttt!*" Matt began to shriek, his voice shifting from a manly baritone to a Maria Callas soprano.

The world spun in slow motion as I noticed four or five soggy spider legs slowly unfolding from the paper towel, a small head with eyes coming back to life like a demented zombie arachnid.

"It's coming *ouuuuuuuttt!!!*" Matt continued to scream, racing toward the trash can and dropping the paper towels from his hand as if they were burning embers from hell's fiery depths.

I grabbed another paper towel and finished the job, assuredly killing the spider with nine lives.

Matt slumped to the floor, exhausted and bewildered.

I slumped beside him. I, too, was out of breath.

Mabel tiptoed into the kitchen, sniffed the trash can, and looked at us with deep doggy concern—and a hint of mocking. We could see her thinking, "Sheeze guys. Next time just put the spider on the floor; I'll flop over and roll it to death just like I do the baby birds in the backyard."

The three of us stared at each other silently until she turned to walk away, clicking her toenails on the ceramic tile in a smarmy, high-heeled, judgmental way.

I glared at Matt.

"What?! It's not my fault."

I knew that, but there are times in our lives when we just need someone to glare at. I sighed, staring at the ceiling, wondering what I'd done to deserve a house full of creepy crawlers. And while I slumped there on the floor, I wondered why Romeo and Juliet had never had to battle roaches. I didn't know why Shakespeare chose to shield his readers from the cold hard facts of life, but it would have been infinitely more helpful if he'd given us a battle plan.

The next day was Sunday and Matt and I went to church. I tried not to think about what our friends would say if they knew about our bug situation. I already had the number for the local pest control company on speed dial, my finger poised and ready for Monday morning so I could set up an appointment.

On the way home from church, while I was fantasizing about the deaths of hundreds of spiders, my cell phone rang. It was Bryan. My stomach knotted instantly.

Angela was in the hospital again. She'd had another surgery a few days earlier to remove the cancerous lesion on her lung and the procedure had not gone well. The surgeon had described the way the rogue tumor broke apart midsurgery. He talked about flushing her chest cavity with water to ensure they got all the cancerous bits out of her, but none of it made us feel better. At the time all I could do was watch her father, Larry, sink into a waiting room chair and put his head in his hands. I sat helplessly, a friend amongst family, trying to fight the feeling of anger lashing up in acidic waves.

Angela had not bounced back from this surgery with her normal spirited spunk. She had not complained about the hospital food, whereas she normally made jokes saying, "One simply cannot be excited about a dinner of beige-colored food with the consistency of wet paper." She had not compared her room to a prison cell built for people unable to outrun the nurses. She didn't turn on the TV. She was silent.

So when my cell phone rang that Sunday morning, I was instantly concerned.

"Liz, hey. Do you think you could stop by the hospital today?" Bryan's voice sounded strained.

"Why? Has something happened?"

"No, it's just . . ." his voice faded out and then he cleared his throat, "I just think it might be good if she had someone to talk to. She's not doing great today."

"I'll be right there," I answered and motioned for Matt to take the hospital exit off the freeway.

As I snapped the phone shut Matt patted my hand.

"Did something happen?"

"I don't know."

It wasn't like Bryan to ask for help. He soldiered on stoically, hardly ever asking for assistance when it came to her illness. He, like Angela, strove with every ounce of his being to keep the people he cared about from being inconvenienced. I knew full well that if Bryan was worried, much less asking me for help, there was something terribly wrong.

We parked the car and I practically sprinted through the hospital. When we got to her room the afternoon sun shone through the blinds in narrow slats, dust particles sparkled in the air like glitter. Angela's eyes were closed, and Bryan stood at the end of her bed, watching.

A roar of panic filled my ears. Had they found another tumor? Was it pneumonia? The doctors had warned it was a possibility.

I heard Matt asking Bryan about getting some coffee downstairs and then they were gone. Angela opened her eyes. Her nose was red. She'd been crying.

"Hey." I perched on the side of her bed. "Bryan called. What's going on?"

She shook her head, her eyes welling up with tears. "Today was the first day I realized I might not beat this."

I took a deep breath and stared out the window. This was the moment I had dreaded. This was the moment Bryan had dreaded. This was why he called me. Not because I could help, but because he didn't know what to say. And truthfully, I didn't either. Neither one of us wanted to discuss the reality of the situation.

"I woke up this morning and realized that it's me and the cancer. I'm alone in this."

I shook my head. "Come on. This doesn't sound like the stubborn fighting woman I know." I wanted to kick myself for responding like a lame football coach trying to pep up a room full of adolescent boys on homecoming night, but it was the only thing I could think to say.

Angela turned to face me. I noticed the dark circles under her eyes. "Liz, this woman is really, really tired."

I reached out and gripped her hand. We sat in silence. Finally, she spoke again.

"I appreciate the cards. The prayers. The visits. I appreciate the 'We're going to beat this' speeches from the doctors and surgeons. Everyone means well. But in the end, there is no 'we.' And this morning when I woke up I was all alone with this cancer. And I realized this could be it."

I swallowed hard. I had taken for granted that she would never be anything less than strong, sensible Angela. I hadn't considered that everyone, even someone as stoic and centered and emotionally grounded as Angela, reaches a breaking point.

"What if I never see my little sister become a mom? What if I'm not around to take care of my parents when they get old? What happens to Bryan . . ." Her voice broke.

I swallowed a sob.

"What if I reach the end and I haven't been a good enough person? What if God looks at me and says, 'Nice try.'" She tried to smile, tried to play it off like a joke, but she wasn't joking.

"That's not possible." I found myself suddenly very angry. Angry at myself for not being better prepared. I wished I were a theologian or a Bible scholar, or at the very least someone smarter who knew the right thing to say. I knew that her mom and sister and best friend Kate, all hundreds of miles away, might better be able to comfort her. They might have the right words. But I didn't. The weight of it all was heavy on my chest.

"If God doesn't love you . . . then the rest of us are in a lot of damn trouble."

Angela laughed suddenly, wiping her eyes. "You do realize you just mentioned the Lord and Savior and profanity within the same sentence."

I shook my head. "I'm sorry. My words aren't coming out like I wish they would today."

She leaned her head back, gazing out the window again. "I find you perfectly eloquent."

The hum of the window fan kicked on, fluttering an arrangement of peace lilies in the corner.

"You've been married a good while now. You and Matt love each other. Why don't you have children?" Her eyes were teary in the sunlight as she stared at me.

I shrugged, taken aback by the directness of her question. "I don't know. A lot of reasons. Too busy. Not enough money. Not sure I'd be good at it."

She nodded, turning back to gaze into the dusty sunlight. "It was always the same for me. I never really wanted children. I was so much older than my sister, in some ways it felt like I helped raise Anna. I felt like I'd already done the parenting thing. I wanted to make money, travel, enjoy my marriage. But yesterday, yesterday . . ."

Her voice trailed off. The food cart rolled past loudly as someone in the hallway whistled.

She cleared her throat. "Yesterday the doctor sat down with me and told me that children will never be a possibility. He told me that all the drugs and numerous rounds of chemotherapy, and the fact that all these tumors keep popping up . . . I can't do it. He just wanted to be sure I understood. And I never wanted to, not until that moment. And now it's too late."

I stretched out on the edge of the bed, doing my best to put my arms around her despite all the tubes. We lay there in silence, both of us thinking about cancer, the children we didn't have, the children she would never have.

"If I ever get out of this alive, I'm going to do things so differently," she whispered. "I'm going to quit my job. I'm going to finish writing my book. I'm going to take in foster children. I think I'd be good at it. There's more than one way to have a family you know."

I squeezed her tighter. "Absolutely."

"I had so much time before, so many possibilities stretching endlessly ahead of me. But it's not endless. This all has an expiration date."

We lay there in silence until the guys came back. Bryan strode across the room in three giant steps, his eyes brimming with concern for his wife.

"Feeling better?" he asked hopefully.

I felt ashamed I hadn't done a better job. I felt ashamed that he'd called on me to help and all I'd done was cry and lay next to her on a hospital bed.

"I just want our life back," she said as they gazed at each other. The air in the room crackled with the intensity of their love. They saw nothing but each other.

I got up from the bed and squeezed her hand again.

"I love you, Ang."

"I love you, too."

I rode home in silence.

"I'm worried about you," Matt said softly, pushing my hair away from my forehead. "This is a pretty tough business you're dealing with."

I smiled at him, unable to speak. Her words haunted me. The fact that she was considering death haunted me. The children she couldn't have haunted me. When we got home I sat in the library listening to Matt making lunch in the kitchen.

"Do you want mayo or mustard?" he called out.

When Matt worried about people, he fed them. I smiled, thinking of him bustling around in the kitchen, urgent in his task to make me the perfect plate of food, a plate of food that would make me happy and forget my troubles. I loved him for it.

"Mayo, please," I called back.

The afternoon sunlight streamed through the window sheers and across my desk. Out of nowhere, a small black spider scurried across the floor beside my foot. My first reaction was to stomp and squish the creature into oblivion. But instead I just sat there. I watched as it scurried frantically to the safety of a bookshelf. I no longer wanted to annihilate every spider in existence. I didn't want anything to die.

Angela's words had shifted something deep inside me. I knew that before that morning I had no true plans to pursue a career as a writer. It was just a hobby, a childhood dream, like becoming a ballerina or a jungle explorer. Earlier that morning I had no urge to have a family. And yet as we drove away from the hospital, I had watched the side of Matt's face and something inside me had changed forever. God willing, I would write a book. Someday we would have a family. I would do it for her. I would do it for me.

CHAPTER 9

The Case of the Scaredy-Matt

December 25, 1962

Dear Dad & Hannah,

It is my first Christmas away from home as a married woman, and I must say, I miss you terribly.

Ned & I arrived at his parents' yesterday afternoon. I cannot believe his parents moved to Little Rock. I realize that his father was born here and has always dreamed of moving back to his hometown. But I must say it's odd down here.

The flight was long and bumpy. We were crammed into a small plane that the stewardess jokingly referred to as a "puddle jumper" over the PA system. I wasn't amused. Frankly, it would not have surprised me to have seen a crate of goats in the back and small children riding in the overhead luggage compartments.

A man across the aisle asked me, "Are y'all Yankees?" To which I replied, "Sir, I am an American." Ned elbowed me and told me I was being a snob. But it's fairly hard not to experience a bad attitude and culture shock while riding next to a woman whose T-shirt reads, "One Tequila, Two Tequila, Three Tequila, Floor."

His parents picked us up at the airport, and it's always so nice to see Mother and Father Nickerson.

They have purchased a colonial-style home similar to our own, except their shutters are red instead of blue. Their choice of holiday decor, however, was a bit unexpected. Again, Ned told me not to be a snob. But it's difficult not to be disconcerted when you face a Christmas with a fake tree and a light-up plastic Santa swathed in a rebel flag.

I inquired about the use of the Confederate flag (something I see frequently in yards around the neighborhood).

Father Nickerson responded, "Nancy, that's the flag we flew during the War of Northern Aggression."

I stared at him blankly. "You mean the Civil War?"

"Yes. That's an emblem of our Southern pride."

To which I replied, "I thought it was an emblem of slavery and oppression?"

Father Nickerson is now in the process of not speaking to me.

Around lunchtime I began helping Mother Nickerson as she prepared Christmas dinner. I was quite upset to find there will be no holiday ham, green bean casserole, or Hannah's lovely pink Jell-O salad. Instead, Mother Nickerson informed me that their family has squash casserole, chocolate cake, and a deep-fried turkey. This distressed me greatly, as you know how partial I am to our normal Christmas traditions. After all, how can it possibly be the holiday season with sixty-degree temperatures, the distant hum of four-wheelers, and giant fried birds? Christmas means the smell of evergreens, the crisp chill of white snow, the aroma of Hannah's baking wafting into the *dining room where our chandelier is bedecked with holly and ornaments.*

But, I digress.

I watched with great trepidation as Mother and Father Nickerson set up the "turkey fry" on the front yard. They used a giant vat of hot oil beside the front porch. It seemed to me an unsafe location, and so I spoke up.

"Perhaps we should fry the turkey in the middle of the driveway?"

Father Nickerson patted me on the head (the first time he had spoken to me since I inadvertently blasphemed against the Confederacy). "Oh, Nancy, just sit back and watch the magic, poor girl. You can't help it if you weren't raised right up there in Yankeeland. We'll get you educated if it's the last thing we do."

I bit my lip, not mentioning that I had graduated from college with a 4.0 and did not need further education. After all, I am trying my best not to be a snob.

Father Nickerson, garbed in overalls, affixed the turkey on a wire from the end of his fishing pole. We all watched as he lowered the turkey into the vat. However, as I would later learn, Father Nickerson had overlooked the vital step of thawing the turkey first.

A fireball erupted as the turkey plunged beneath the oil, golden red flames whooshing high in the air. Father Nickerson was saved only because of his distance with the fishing pole. As he flung himself backward and Mother Nickerson's screams filled the air, I watched the angry fireball lash sideways, licking the Confederate garbed Santa and melting it into a small, charred mound of plastic.

In short, the turkey was unable to be salvaged. We made an emergency trip to the butcher shop for a precooked turkey while Father Nickerson attended to a small burn on his left arm.

Things are not boding well.

That night I also learned that Mother Nickerson did not have a proper guest room. Father Nickerson had turned one into a pool table room (complete with his beer can collection), and Mother Nickerson had converted the last remaining guest room into her art studio. Therefore, Ned and I learned we would be sleeping on separate twin blow-up mattresses in the living room. Needless to say, there is a lack of privacy and comfort on this vacation.

As it turned out, my air mattress gradually lost air throughout the night and this morning I awoke in the shape of a human taco, my bottom touching the ground, and the rest of my body enfolded in the semi-inflated mattress. I must admit I panicked and flailed around for several minutes, disoriented, neck aching, all legs and arms, trying my best to get out but only managing to look like a beached whale. Ned awoke and helped me out.

Finally, when I was on my feet, I pushed the hair from my face and said, "I'm not being a snob. But I really prefer to sleep in a motel next time."

And now, as I'm writing this letter to you, Father Nickerson is blasting a George Jones Christmas album from the Hi-Fi,

Mother Nickerson is weeping softly over the loss of her plastic Southern pride Santa, and Ned is taking his third nap of the day. I miss you both.

Love,
Nancy Drew-Nickerson

When it comes to holiday traditions, there are just two ways to do things.

> **1. There is the way you grew up doing it**—"it" being Halloween, Christmas, Easter, or whatever holidays were important to your family. The way you grew up doing it is always perfect, comforting, and right.

> **2. And then there is the way everyone else in the world does it.** Those holiday traditions are completely offensive, wrong, and at times, blasphemous.

Angela and I found that we agreed on one particular holiday issue: We loved Halloween more than Christmas. We cherished the fall colors, the cheerful orange flicker of jack-o-lanterns, the costumes, and the laughing children who spread across the neighborhood on their mission for candy. My deep abiding love for Halloween revolved around the fact that Halloween was always a stress-free holiday. As a child I could remember crisp weather and the score of

Arsenic and Old Lace filling the air as my mom lit candles and made cookies in the shape of Frankenstein's head. It was a holiday that didn't involve worrying about money for presents or travel. It was just my family hanging orange twinkle lights and decorating cookies.

It's not that I don't like Christmas, I like it just fine. It's just a bit of a consolation prize to soothe the fact that I have to take down my fall wreaths and paper door skeleton.

Angela, on the other hand, didn't care for Christmas at all.

"Why?" I asked point blank one chilly December afternoon. We were on our lunch break together and I was shopping for turquoise glass ornaments.

She shrugged, pulling her coat tighter. She was cold. Chemo takes its toll, especially during the colder months. "I just don't care for it. It depresses me. You know that song, 'Have Yourself a Merry Little Christmas?'"

I nodded.

"That song fairly sums up my entire dislike for Christmas. Unnecessarily overdramatic and depressing."

I nodded. We were all entitled to our own holiday opinions. After all, I was the woman who watched the movie *Hocus Pocus* at least five times every October. Who was I to throw stones?

"Why do you go to church, Liz?"

I paused, taken aback by the giant jump in our conversation. Angela seemed to be doing this more and more lately, asking random questions. I didn't know what to say. I didn't understand the random questions on theology falling from the sky, but I knew that facing chemo and your own mortality could do that: create a spinning vortex of deep thoughts spiraling constantly, popping up at unexpected times. Unanswerable questions are easy to avoid for those of us not getting radiated or hacked on; we merely push them into the recesses of our brains and go clean the kitchen. But when you have cancer, I guess you lose that luxury.

Her question hung in the air. *Why do you go to church, Liz?*

My brain scrambled for the right words to say, the right protocol. Somewhere in my life I was sure I'd read a pamphlet on this question, but for the life of me I couldn't remember anything about it. My brow furrowed as I panicked, unsure how to respond.

Angela laughed. "It's a fairly straightforward question."

Suddenly, I realized I didn't have to recite a pamphlet. I could just be honest.

"To tell the truth, for most of my adult life I've gone to church because I was afraid of what it would mean if I didn't."

Angela nodded solemnly. "And now?"

"I go now because . . . I think God might actually be up there. I think he might be watching us after all."

I waited for her to be shocked at my lack of faith. But instead she smiled and nodded.

She picked up a star tree topper and put it back down. "I like going to St. Luke's on Sundays. I feel better when I leave, you know? Besides, I prefer high church, none of that loosey-goosey carrying on in the aisles or rock bands in the front. I think if I'm going to worship the Creator of all that is, I don't intend to do it wallowing on the floor."

I grinned at her and she just smiled, turning to walk ahead of me. Trying to imagine Angela wallowing anywhere, much less on the floor, was like trying to picture Myrna Loy participating in an all-you-can-eat burrito buffet.

I pushed the cart toward the register, and just before we left, Judy Garland's voice echoed through the store, encouraging us all to have a merry little Christmas.

"See what I mean?" Angela huffed indignantly as we exited to the parking lot. "Depressing."

That night I went home to add the finishing touches to our Christmas tree. An old black-and-white movie played on TV. I lit a cinnamon candle. I thought about the incredible standards we all hold ourselves to when it comes to the holidays: the pressure, the unbending traditions, the unrealistic ideals. I'm no different than anyone else. For years I was ashamed as I read blogs and magazines and saw other women drying orange slices for tree ornaments and hanging real, delicious-smelling garlands on their front porch rails. These same women made homemade snow globes, baked pies for their neighbors, and threw expansive holiday feasts. Every year I put up a fake tree that tilts slightly to the right and stuff all the Christmas presents into gift bags with wadded tissue paper on top.

In a way I admired Angela for her heretical opinions about Christmas. Magazines told us to love it, work for it, perfect it. Classic literature was filled with tales of pheasant banquets and elaborate cakes and an Old Saint Nick wearing real fur. It was refreshing to realize that maybe we didn't all have to buy into those pressures.

Most traditions seem insignificant. Insignificant, that is, until someone tries to change them, and then the battle lines are drawn. We fight over whether to open presents on the twenty-fourth or twenty-fifth of December. We are chastised for suggesting that the family draw names instead of buying 148 Christmas presents for the entire extended family. We frown and cross our arms in disapproval as our neighbor puts up the tree *before* Thanksgiving. We can't comprehend why our spouse didn't bake a cake and put up balloons for our birthday. We insist on programming our cell phone ring tone to "Shrieks of Horror" on the first of October despite the fact that our significant other finds the entire holiday morally offensive. It's a veritable minefield.

In my family we have our own set of die-hard, holiday traditions. On Christmas we have ham instead of turkey. My uncle is a retired fireman and insists we all have fake trees so our houses don't burn down (although truthfully, I've yet to meet someone who lost his or her home to a real Christmas tree fire). But one tradition in particular extended outside the boundaries of Halloween and into the rest of the year: My family likes to scare people.

On our first Christmas together as a married couple I hung ornaments, cranked Bing Crosby music, and waited for Matt to get home from work. I thought wistfully about my childhood. If I'd been home, someone would have jumped out from the dark kitchen and shrieked, "Boo!"

Growing up, my sisters and I took turns jumping out of closets yelling, "Gotcha." My father used to prank us with the fuse switches in the basement; reducing whatever room we were playing in to blackness while yowling ghostly noises up the laundry chute. We watched scary movies and donned monkey masks and vampire teeth and terrified each other with stories of swinging treetop creatures that peered into open windows at night. It happened all year long, spring or summer, day or night.

It wasn't until I got married that I realized the odd nature of my family's gleeful scaring sprees.

"That's just weird," Matt had once declared.

On that first Christmas I hung the last ornament and checked my watch. It was 10:00 p.m., and Matt was working late. I lounged on the couch, admiring my ornament-hanging handiwork. And as always, my grandmother's sage logic proved true. Idle hands truly are the devil's playground, because it was at this particular juncture that I decided to induct Matt into the family tradition of spooking.

I heard a car pull into the drive, so I crept over and hid directly behind the front door. I heard his keys jingle outside and the latch snap as he opened the door.

I waited until he shut the door and seized my opportunity. I jumped from the dark corner, fingers curled like claws, and made a catlike sound. "Hissss!"

What happened afterward shocked me. I was used to family members being momentarily stunned and then laughing, slapping their knees and saying, "I'm gonna really get you next time."

That. Is. Not. What. Happened.

My lovely, strong, handsome new husband leaped backwards, belting out the loudest roar I'd ever heard. It went something like this, "*ARIRGHGHGHGHGHGHGIIIIRGHGHGH AAARIRIGHG.*"

And while he was emitting his shriek of horror, he simultaneously threw his keys. I'm not sure why. He didn't throw them at me, but he vaulted them as a projectile object all the way through the living room and into the kitchen at the back of the house. Pure horror causes people to do strange things.

I immediately knew I had made a mistake, ceased hissing, and stood still, hands at my side, eyes wide.

Matt slumped against a chair, exhausted from his massive adrenaline-induced fight-or-flight reaction. "Why would you do that?"

I bit my lip. "I thought it would be funny?"

Matt stared at me silently, obviously rethinking his legal commitments to a complete psycho bride.

I dug a deeper hole. "We do it all the time at home . . . it's fun?"

"Please don't ever do that to me again," Matt said.

"Okay," I promised.

Honestly, looking back, I still feel guilty about that ordeal. I realize it made a sad picture: my poor, foot-weary, hardworking husband, coming home to a weird crouching wife, waiting in the dark to scare the life out of him. I know . . . horrible . . . but it seemed like fun to me at the time.

As it turns out, everyone feels differently when it comes to traditions. Whether it's how you celebrate the holidays, which church you go to, or the proper way to fold bath towels, we're all influenced by deeply entrenched childhood preferences and family customs. Matt preferred his Christmases filled with hot chocolate and *Christmas Vacation* marathons. Angela didn't care for sad Judy Garland songs and churches that mimicked rock concerts. And I, I loved the thrill of scaring the pants off people. It didn't mean any one of us was wrong; it just meant we had to learn to live in a way that promoted love and harmony . . . not cursing and thrown keys.

Maybe that's not the way they did things at Green Gables, but for the first time in a long time, I didn't mind that my literary friends probably had magazine-worthy holidays complete with duck and handmade cranberry garlands for their aromatic spruce trees. I didn't mind that I was forging holiday traditions that deviated from the classic mistletoe and good cheer, or that we spent that holiday season basking in the glow of our fake tree, which Matt refers to as "Big Plastic." Holidays may not transpire as we think they ought to, but we're making our own rules under our own roof.

Oh, and I'd like to say that our house is a boo-free zone, but I still like to dole out a good scare. And since Matt is off-limits, I save all my spooking energy for Mabel. When I jump out from behind a closet door and yell "gotcha" at her, she gets it. She runs in circles barking, wagging her tail while Matt silently shakes his head.

CHAPTER 10

The Renovation of the House of Usher

Roderick paced quickly back and forth across the parlor floor. The cold stone walls of the house chilled him to the bone. He pulled his coat tighter, readjusting his scarf and wishing for the thousandth time for central heat.

"We've got to do something about this place, Mads. Usher Manor needs a serious renovation. This place is falling down around our ears."

Madeline smiled at her brother, the eerie smile that generally disconcerted everyone who met her, a half smile, half growl. Roderick assumed that his sister merely ground her teeth at night and had perhaps popped her jaw out of place.

"Roderick, I don't think we need to do anything. The house is just fine." She pulled the quilt off the back of the sofa and wrapped it around her feet.

Roderick pursed his lips, fighting the urge to roll his eyes. He knew perfectly well his strange sister would be at peace living with one candle and a thousand spiderwebs hanging all over her bedroom.

"But just look at this place!" He couldn't contain himself anymore, gazing up at the chandelier overhead. "Look at the decor in here! It looks like a flashback to the middle ages. The

fluorescent lighting in the basement is hideously bright; I prac-
tically have to wear sunglasses when I'm down there. And
don't even get me started on the dishwasher in the kitchen. It
barely gets our stemware clean anymore, and . . ."

Madeline's eyes narrowed beneath her long lashes. *"Don't*
raise your voice at me, Roderick. I don't like it."

"Sure, sure," he muttered, glancing at her in alarm. Mads
had a tendency to shriek like a cat and claw his face when she
was upset. It wasn't exactly normal for a woman in her station,
but Roderick just attributed it to PMS.

"All I'm saying is, I'd commit murder for a brand-new side-
by-side fridge. You know, the kind with a clear glass front?
Those are heavenly."

"I say we wait for a sign!" Madeline giggled hysteri-
cally, always in possession of a flair for the weird and dra-
matic. "Let's wait for something spooky to happen, something
scarrryyyy."

She giggled again and Roderick moved farther away, eye-
ing her with careful alarm. There were many times he'd teased
his sister in the past, he had even told her she'd been left on
their doorstep by trolls. But back then she'd been too little to
hurt him. She certainly wasn't too little now.

Oh, how he wished his parents had made arrangements
for his "special" sister before they had died, like marrying her
off to a rich landowner with a ready supply of straitjackets.
Frankly, he was tired of telling his coworkers he'd cut himself
shaving instead of telling them the truth, which was that he
burned Mads's toast and she lit into him with her fingernails

like a psychopathic squirrel. And there was no way he could ever bring a date home with her still living in the house, skulking inexplicably in dark corners and spitting her chewed fingernail pieces at strangers.

"Listen!" Madeline sat upright, clutching her quilt, a feverish glow of excitement in her eyes. "Did you hear that? Someone's here!"

Roderick tilted his head to listen, and sure enough there were three sharp raps on the front door.

"Shhh . . . wait here." He jumped up, peering nervously out the window. The night was dark as pitch, so he moved cautiously into the foyer, relieved to see he'd bolted the front doors. His shoes clicked as he passed over the marble floors and cracked open the door.

"Hello?" he called into the night air. There was nothing there, just blackness before him.

"That's curious," he said.

And then he looked downward.

Perched on the top step of the porch was a small black raven.

"Well, hello there, Mr. Raven." Roderick couldn't help but smile as the bird hopped cheerfully through the open door and into the foyer.

Roderick had always fancied the idea of having a pet. But, alas, with Madeline it was nearly impossible. They had once had a sheepdog named Poopsie. Madeline had shaved every hair Poopsie had off his body, and so Poopsie went to live with a nice family on a farm nearby. At twelve Roderick was given two gerbils. Madeline began feeding them a steady diet of steak and chocolate cake until they reached a weight far surpassing fat and into the gigantic circus-freak category. They too went to live with the nice farm family.

After years of pet deprivation, Roderick found himself enamored with the concept of owning a living thing. As he gazed at the bird, he realized Mr. Raven might just suit the bill.

Madeline scuttled from the parlor, wrapped in a quilt, her wild hair sticking out in all directions. But Mr. Raven seemed impervious to her startling appearance as he turned and examined her.

"I think it's a sign, Mads!" Roderick clasped his hands. "He looks like he's going to speak!"

Madeline hid partly behind a support column, watching the bird suspiciously with one eye.

"Blerrrkkk," Mr. Raven croaked, clearing its throat.

"What is it friend? Give us your message." Roderick kneeled down, aware that his sister was gazing at him as if he possessed three heads. But he didn't care. He had a strange feeling that this bird was about to solve all of his problems.

"Kenmore," blurted Mr. Raven.

"Come again?" Roderick whispered back.

"Kenmore," Mr. Raven stated simply.

Roderick clapped his hands excitedly, "Did you hear that, Mads?"

Madeline nodded, wary of the strange talking bird and her exuberant brother.

"Hahaha!" Roderick laughed loudly and began to skip around the room. "It's the sign we needed! Our renovation is

fate! And our fate lies in a brand-new side-by-side fridge with matching dishwasher from Kenmore!"

"Kenmore," agreed Mr. Raven.

"Now wait a minute, Rod." Madeline held up her hands, inexperienced at being the rational sibling. "Let's think this over. It will be very expensive, and you seem a little overwrought."

"Kenmore," insisted Mr. Raven.

"I'm not overwrought!" Roderick shouted and spun, arms outstretched with joy. "It's just renovation fever, Mads! It happens to everyone!"

"Kenmore," agreed Mr. Raven.

"And Kenmore it shall be!" Roderick skipped down the main hall, lightning illuminating the windows as Mr. Raven hopped after him, repeating his one word message.

"Kenmore it is." Madeline sighed in resignation.

Renovation fever. It's a state of mind that overtakes perfectly rational, frugal people and turns them into marble-countertop–hunting, wall-smashing, chandeliers-in-every-room fiends. This type of fever is actually a distant cousin to the Zombie Virus that is spread through the act of biting. But Renovation Fever is spread through the act of visiting the bigger and better homes of your neighbors and feeling like a gigantic loser stuck with linoleum floors.

When Matt and I bought our first house, we gave tours as cheerfully and proudly as a pair of lady civic leaders during a holiday tour of homes. Never mind the fact that our popcorn ceilings were only partially scraped. Never mind the fact that we had only 1,400 square feet and a tiny closet for the washer/dryer. Never mind that the roof shingles were harvest gold and the grout lines were chipping in the kitchen. We were proud. And when you're proud, you give tours, whether people want to go on them or not.

"You don't want to see our retro paneled guest room? Too bad. Get over here now."

We were prepared to live with the faux wood floors in the den. We didn't give a second thought to the wobbly drawers in the kitchen. What we weren't prepared for were the naysayers, the homeowners who had already succumbed to Renovation Fever and were rabidly trying to pass it on.

I remember the first time we were infected.

Mr. Renovator eyed our tiny L-shaped kitchen with a critical eye. "You know, instead of ripping out these cabinets, I'd do something a little cheaper."

I began blinking rapidly like a confused Betty Boop doll with open-close eyes. "Who said anything about ripping out cabinets?"

Mr. Renovator ignored me. "I'd just replace all the drawer and cabinet fronts. That'll save you a ton of money."

I examined our dilapidated 1952 cabinets and tried not to stick out my bottom lip. "You know what else saves a ton of money?"

"What?" Mr. Renovator was genuinely interested.

"Leaving a perfectly decent kitchen alone."

Normally, that kind of response would be enough to stop an uncomfortable conversation in its tracks, but victims of Renovation Fever know no bounds when it comes to converting people to their cult of "I Ripped All the Carpeting Out of My House Because I Didn't Like the Color Beige."

Mr. Renovator shrugged tolerantly. "Let's go look at the bathroom."

I groaned and trailed behind him, shooting Matt a glance that said, "Clunk him over the head with something and do it quick. The bathroom will put him over the edge and he'll try to rip the tiles out with his fingernails."

Matt shot me a look that said, "Just nod your head and he'll leave soon."

Matt and I have telepathic abilities during times of extreme emotional stress. We're like a psychic Nick and Nora.

And so Mr. Renovator peered past the doorway into our small, 1950s, Mamie Pink–tile bathroom. I closed my eyes, waiting for the nuclear fallout.

"Well." He gulped and finally mustered the ability to speak. "You know . . . you can always paint the tile."

My windpipe closed in on itself. "Why would we ever do that?"

Mr. Renovator laughed huffily like Einstein speaking to a lowly preschooler. "Obviously, when it comes to resale of this house, no one will want to buy a bathroom like that."

"I did!" I snarled darkly, prickling at the idea of anyone not loving the pink tiles that hearkened back to my grandmother's era of *Leave It to Beaver* and Jell-O mold salads.

"Listen, I don't want to pick a fight. You've got good bones in this place. But no one buys their dream home. You have to make it. Surely you have a dream home? Well, just put that in your mind when you're remodeling the one you have."

We watched him leave with crossed arms. But what he'd said had planted a tiny seed in my mind. A microscopic germ. A baby version of Renovation Fever. And as the days passed, I felt it festering. I thought once again of my dream home, and in my mind's eye, I began to see all kinds of home improvement possibilities. Visions of beadboard, porches, and farmhouse sinks began to dance in my head. I didn't realize I had been infected until one peaceful February day. The weather was oddly warm, and a balmy breeze blew across the yard as Matt and I worked and swept out the carport.

"We should paint the house," Matt mentioned casually. "I think gray brick would look great."

"Absolutely!" I jumped in with both feet, thrilled that the metaphorical renovation door had been opened. "That will look great, especially one day when we build on the second story."

"What?" Matt's forehead wrinkled in concern.

"You know, when we add on a second story and a wrap-around porch, to make it look more like a farmhouse."

Matt blinked slowly before setting aside his rake. "I have no idea what you're talking about."

Suddenly I realized I'd never bothered to share my Anne of Green Gables master plan with him. I do this sometimes. I have very vivid, elaborate, hand-waving, dual conversations between myself and other people, completely within the privacy of my own head. I may not have directly told Matt about my dream home, Liz Gables, or my plans to one day fly airplanes and go on safari with a Clark Gable look-alike, and yet, I had. It gets very confusing, mostly for Matt.

"Well," I hedged, "I just figured that with your job, and my job, we'll never get a chance to live in the country and refurbish an old farmhouse. So, we can just remodel this one. Eventually, of course."

This is the point at which most husbands would delve into a lecture, detailing their argument in outline form to logically persuade their wife that her idea is silly and unreasonable. But Matt likes to keep things simple.

"Liz. No."

The word *no,* for me personally, is the verbal equivalent of waving a red flag in front of a bull, or in my case, a flag of rejection momentarily blocking my view of Green Gables.

"Carrie thought it was a good idea."

Carrie is my best friend from childhood. She also humors me by telling me that every idea I have is a good one. Because that's what true friends do. They lie to make you happy.

Matt pursed his lips. "No. We can't afford it."

"We could eventually!" I insisted, ready to protect my literary dream home like a mother bear defending a cub. But as I began a long and complicated verbal defense of said dream, the shield of silence clamped itself across Matt's face. So I switched tactics.

"Didn't you ever have a dream home as a child?"

Matt was stony. "No. When I was little I read *The Call of the Wild* and slept in the backyard in a tent."

I saw my opening and jumped through. "Well, this can work out for you too. You can fulfill your dream when we gut the bottom floor and add a staircase. We'll camp in the backyard in a tent while the contractor works. And you know how the neighbors' dogs howl when the police sirens go off? You can pretend they're wolves."

"You're nuts," Matt stated matter-of-factly as he turned and walked away.

I shrugged, returning my gaze to our humble ranch abode. "That's probably what they told Frank Lloyd Wright."

And so I stood by as my neighbors installed granite countertops and built sunrooms onto the backs of their houses. I watched *This Old House* and glowed green with envy as homeowners put in new floors, built back stairwells in their kitchens, and reused old transom windows in custom-built doorways.

No matter where I looked, I was dissatisfied. My house, which had not so long ago charmed me with its bouncy pier-and-beam flooring and uneven walls, now elicited a feeling of distrust. And so I brewed, stewed, and walked around in a fog of general discontent.

A few weeks later my cell phone rang on a dark and stormy night. It was Carrie. In addition to having grown up together, we were now lucky enough to live in the same town.

Carrie and I had braved the perils of the dreaded teenage years together. We'd gone through many phases while searching for ourselves and how we fit into the world. These phases involved singing at county fairs, a short stint where we wore the dreaded, figure-killing Wrangler jeans, and a small span of time when we double-dated a pair of boys who took us on a "date" that involved slow dancing in the back of a pickup truck in a cow field. Luckily, those days were behind us and we were loyal enough to bury the picture evidence deep within our attic trunks.

"Hey! Have you been watching the news?"

I had not. There were storm warnings across the state and yet I was so deeply immersed in Renovation Fever, all I could do was sit and stare at the space in the wall where a stairwell should be while mumbling, "All work and no construction makes Liz a pissed off girl."

Carrie's voice shook with panic. "They say Mountain View took a direct tornado hit."

Our childhood hometown, Mountain View, Arkansas, is a sleepy Ozark community tucked into the hills, steeped in folk music, mud flaps, overalls, and a healthy fear of outsiders. But it is home. We love it. My feelings toward Mountain View have always been similar to the way I feel about my family. Sure, they may spit snuff in plastic cups and fight tooth and nail over their belief that Hank Williams Sr. could have overtaken Elvis in a cage match. But while I feel I'm allowed to laugh at them, I tend to bristle when others snicker, point, and hum the theme song from *Deliverance*.

Immediately I hung up and dialed my parents' phone number. A mechanical automated female voice droned, "The number you have dialed is unavailable."

I paced back and forth across the living room as a clap of thunder rattled the walls. The phone lines were down. I thought of my parents, a mere two hours away, huddled in a house on the edge of a cliff, in the middle of the mountains, all alone in a violent storm. I panicked.

During the next few hours I wore the print off my pointer finger, repeatedly dialing and hanging up, trying again and again as the infuriating recording repeated its message in my ear. Carrie continued to call, unable to reach her family either.

The news was sketchy. Reporters said the road to Mountain View was cut off and it was impossible to assess exactly how severe and widespread the damage was until dawn. When tornadoes form over mountains, they don't behave the same way they do over flat ground. They tend to bounce from mountain to mountain, traveling long distances like demented, spinning tops.

As the night wore on, we finally received a text message from my parents. "We're safe, house is fine, town hit, county out of power, cell towers messed up."

The relief I felt was indescribable, but Carrie's news was not good. Her extended family's farm had been hit.

Matt often jokes to his friends that he married a redneck. I've often corrected him, snapping, "We're hill people! There's a difference!" But perhaps he's right. It's strange how the culture you're raised in seems to come back to you in times of stress and catastrophe. I often watch disasters on the news and lecture the city dwellers around me, a hint of my Ozark accent creeping in: "What those people really need are some good four-wheelers and a wrench to clear the rubble."

And so, in the spirit of our redneck upbringing, Carrie and I sprung to action and set off to check on her family—her car loaded with water, blankets, tape, flashlights, and food.

Our drive through the winding mountain highways was eerie as each of us noted no passing traffic to or from Mountain View. It felt like we were the only vehicle on Earth. As we approached the city limits, we grew quiet. There are some life events so shocking they render even talkative, yappy gals like us into silence. This was one of them.

Giant trees lay across garages, houses sloped and leaned like a Hollywood movie set, power lines dangled and swayed from snapped poles. We passed a few people we knew, waving to a friend's grandfather as he wielded a chain saw, cutting a tree from the top of his truck.

The damage in town became more dramatic: tossed cars swinging from the tops of trees, the firehouse leveled, the press box at the high school football field askew and hanging off the bleachers. The hospital was annihilated.

We continued farther down a highway and turned onto the gravel road that led to Carrie's family farm.

The farm had been in her family for many generations, a piece of valley land between two babbling creeks, sweeping bluffs and fertile green fields on either side. Her great-great-grandfather had come over from Ireland, built the house, and started a farm that had lasted for centuries.

Thankfully, neighbors with chain saws had cleared a path for us to pass through, but as we drove toward the family farm, we both cried out. The old house, which had endured the Civil War, the Great Depression, two world wars, and countless generations of Carrie's family, was in a condemned state. Giant chunks of the roof were missing, the front porch sagged, the entire frame shifted slightly off the foundation. Windows with original glass were blown out, pipes broken, and hallways twisted like a funhouse.

We jumped from the car and stood staring up at the house. Carrie's cousins, aunts, uncles, and parents buzzed around, busying themselves with the cleanup.

"Hey there, girls!" A family friend waved to us as she unfolded a bright orange tarp. "It's one heck of a way to redecorate," she grinned, pointing to the tarp, "but I've always found myself partial to the color orange. We're using these on our roof too."

She went on to explain that her own house had sustained extensive damage as well.

"I'm so sorry," Carrie said.

She shook her head grinning. "Everything's okay. Hell, honey, we ain't dead!"

As I stood there, watching them spread the orange tarp over the roof of the decimated home, I thought of my time spent in metaphorical sackcloth and ashes, mulling over imaginary farmhouses and griping about staircases. I was ashamed of myself.

Carrie's relatives were hard at work, drinking coffee brewed on camping stoves, laughing, and hefting chain saws on their backs. Cold, early spring winds swept off the blue-tinged mountains and down the valley, ruffling the roof panels swinging in the trees. Chickens without coops clucked across the yard. It was a scene that should have involved wailing and sorrow, but instead, these people were okay.

Or perhaps better yet, they were thankful. Thankful to be alive, to be together, to have escaped the devastation of a natural disaster. I thought such peace of mind and cheerfulness came from having all your ducks in a row, receiving a windfall inheritance, getting hired for the perfect job, or decorating the perfect house. I thought the stars must align for it to occur. And for the first time, I realized that wasn't the case at all.

We spent the day emptying the demolished house, carefully stepping over glass and cracks in floors. It felt good to be useful. Before we left town we stopped to say hello to my parents and sister Rachel, who were cleaning out the yard of a church member.

Our drive back home was a quiet one as Carrie and I remained deep in thought about the devastation we'd just seen. When I arrived home and unlocked the door, I felt a much different emotion. I wasn't quite as horrified by the chipped Formica countertops. I shrugged at the tiny closets.

A few days later Angela and I attended the Arkansas Home and Garden Show at a downtown convention center.

I described the devastation in Mountain View to her in great detail, and she listened seriously. Our talk then turned to our roses from the previous year and new plans for the spring. A song about limes and drinking from coconuts came on the radio and Angela turned it up louder.

It's safe to say that Angela and I were never big partyers. We never hung over balconies and threw up alcohol and lime concoctions. We never participated in wet T-shirt contests in Florida during spring break. There once was a day I might have done those things, but I had parents who threatened self-combustion. Angela never did those things because her inner compass of Emily Post behavior would never have allowed it. But as we sang loudly in unison about coconuts in anticipation of an entire convention center full of plants and flowers, we were in our own dorky version of party girl mode.

I took a deep breath, looking forward to spring's glorious colors and chirping birds when all at once I realized our car was moving at a brisk pace toward a red light.

"Ummm . . ." was all I got out as Angela zoomed through the intersection without stopping.

"Ang, did you see that red light?" My pasty-pale version of party mode was now gone and forgotten as I sat upright, fingers clenching my knees.

"Oh. Oh! My gosh, I'm sorry!" she yelled, but not before zooming through a second red light.

I began to shriek, which probably didn't help the situation.

Angela's face was ashen as she stomped on the brakes, swerving into a parking lot.

I gulped, fanning my face with the garden show brochure. She just sat there, facing forward, jaw clenched.

"Ang, it's okay. We're okay. Really."

She shook her head slowly. "I have a bad feeling, Liz."

"Why?" I sat upright, immediately alarmed. "Are you feeling sick?"

She stared straight ahead, so deep in thought I knew she was unable to hear me. "Even when I forget for a moment, it's always there."

I started to open my mouth to respond, but instead closed it. I realized that maybe sometimes I didn't need to fill uncomfortable silences with my burbling. Maybe it was a good time to shut up and let her talk.

"It's always on my mind. Every time I look in the mirror I'm reminded of cancer. Every time I watch a funny movie and start laughing, it all comes rushing back. I remember that . . ." her voice cracked. "I remember that my next scan could show more tumors, more cancer. It could be spreading, right now, at this very instant. This time next year I might not be here. I might not be here watching movies or going to a garden show."

We sat staring at the empty Saturday morning downtown parking lot around us. I reached out and turned off the radio. Its cheerful island song was suddenly inappropriate. Angela shifted in her seat, her gaze fixed across the parking lot on the church steeple in the distance.

"I'm sorry about the red lights. I've got another big scan coming up. I start thinking about these things and get so . . . distracted."

I nodded, waiting for her to say more, but she didn't. She didn't want pity. She didn't want to be a cancer patient. She just wanted to be normal. She just wanted to feel alive.

"You are going to beat this," I said. It was just another terribly clichéd response, but I felt it in my bones. I believed with all my heart that if anyone was strong enough to make cancer retreat into the distance, it was Angela.

"All that chemo wiped those cancer cells into oblivion."

She smiled slightly, still gazing at the steeple. Her face seemed to have aged ten years in two minutes.

"And don't worry about the red lights. I know all about being distracted behind the wheel. Did I ever tell you about the time I drove into my house?"

Angela chuckled, the tense flex of her jawline relaxing a little. I smiled back, the knot in my stomach easing. I'd spent my entire life trying to comfort others by embarrassing myself. When my sisters were little girls and crying, I'd slap myself in the head, cry out, and fall to the floor. That always seemed to do the trick. They'd wipe the tears from their red faces and fill the air with their baby laughter. It was worth it, even with the occasional bruise. And as I sat watching Angela, my heart filled with the need to do it all over again.

"It was a really rainy night and my sneakers were soaked. I jumped in the car, drove home, and just as I pulled into the driveway . . . *bam*."

She smiled patiently.

"My foot slipped right off the brake and jammed into the accelerator. Before I knew what was happening the car rammed into the side of the house. It took my uncle two days to rebuild the brick foundation. So, seriously, those red lights? Not nearly as bad."

She started to chuckle softly, nodding her head. There is immeasurable comfort in having a friend who loves you because of, and not in spite of, your spastic, frenzied nature.

"Is any of this blubbering storytime helping?"

She laughed again, only this time it was a real laugh, a loud one that filled the car and lit up her face. "I love you the most when you're telling stories. You remind me of my sister. So tell me, did Matt freak out when you rammed into your house?"

I shrugged. "I think he figured it was par for the course."

"I bet." She took a deep breath, squared her shoulders, and adjusted the white scarf on her head. "Let's go see some flowers then."

The convention center was packed when we arrived. Numerous booths from local florists and landscapers were filled with ornate arrangements, advice brochures, and exotic succulents. As we perused the booths, sniffing flowers and discussing grand plans for our yards, I began to notice something. In each booth, at least one person stopped what they were doing and stared at Ang. At first I dismissed it, but after a few minutes and at least a dozen prolonged stares, it became clear I wasn't being overly sensitive.

While I'd grown accustomed to her scarf-wrapped head, others weren't. I realized that as humans, even the smallest oddity or difference triggers some sort of bell that screams, "Alert! Alert! Something is different about her!" Some of us were raised by mothers who slapped the back of our heads and said, "Don't stare! It's rude." And others, well, others had obviously never learned that lesson.

Truthfully, she didn't need the scarves anymore. Her hair had started to grow beautifully in my opinion. It hung all over her head in very short, perfect ringlets. I thought it looked like Leslie Caron's pixie haircut. But Angela mourned for her long hair and the way she used to look. Every now and then there were days when she still wore the scarves over her head. Those were the days when she was struggling the most. This was one of those days.

I felt a slow burn in the pit of my stomach. Angela examined a purple orchid, face placid as she went about her business. But I knew better. I knew she felt each stare like a dagger in her back. And for a woman whose pride and privacy were the cogs around which her universe turned, it must have felt like walking on hot coals. Why did people care if she wore a scarf on her head? What business was it of theirs?

I took a deep breath, trying to calm myself. After all, some of the stares came accompanied by smiles of pity. They meant well. They were probably thinking, "Oh, poor girl. So young." But I was angry. Angela didn't need their pity.

I stewed silently, doing my best to pretend with Angela that no one noticed the scarf stylishly wrapped around her head. I tried my best to forget that the chemo hadn't blanched her complexion to a translucent pale. But after half an hour, I was raw from the effort. It was at this particular juncture a stranger walked up and examined her intensely. It was on the tip of my tongue, all the anger and fear and frustration I had for her, but he spoke first.

"Excuse me, are you Larry's daughter?"

Surprise registered in her eyes as she nodded.

"My business partner is a good friend of his, and I just wanted you to know how incredibly brave I think you are."

Angela stiffened, unaccustomed to dealing with praise from strangers. I, on the other hand, loved him instantly. I wanted to draw him to one side and say, "Listen, people in here are staring at her. Do you want to walk around with me and knock some heads together?"

"I don't want to interrupt what you were doing, I just wanted to say hello. God bless you, Angela."

And with that, he disappeared into the crowd.

We stood in silence for a moment before she touched my arm. "Do you mind if we leave after the next booth? I'm really tired."

Of course I didn't mind. As I turned to say it, I saw that her face had changed. The guard was gone. The stiff lines eased. Her eyes were smiling. The red lights were forgotten.

I thought of my dream house. I thought of the imaginary renovation that we couldn't afford and didn't need. I pondered Carrie's family, uplifted in the face of great devastation. I gazed at Angela's face, determined and happy, buoyed up by the kind words of a stranger.

When Angela dropped me off at the house, I turned and hugged her.

"What was that for?"

"I love you, and I'm just . . . just . . . so sorry . . . for all of this."

"Why?" Her laugh filled the car. "You didn't give me cancer, what do you have to be sorry for? Anyway, didn't you hear? I've been blessed."

I smiled back the tears and got out of the car. I marched into the house, grabbed Matt, and kissed him with a fervor he hadn't seen since the inception of my renovation obsession.

"Whoa!" He grinned, hugging me back tightly. "What's all this?"

"Nothing, I just decided our ranch house is just fine. I don't need a renovation."

He squinted at me suspiciously. "Who are you and what did you do with Liz?"

I didn't respond. I just kissed him again. I've found that's the best possible way to distract a man and simultaneously communicate a sincere apology without actually having to say it aloud.

You see, there's nothing wrong with remodeling a kitchen or putting beadboard in a bathroom. There is intrinsic joy in pruning, editing, and transforming the homes we live in. But sometimes, we need to learn lessons from tornado survivors who remain upbeat and determined. Sometimes we need to allow ourselves to be blessed by perfect strangers. And sometimes we need to stand proudly in our outdated kitchen, forget about our Renovation Fever, and kiss our husbands.

CHAPTER 11

The House of Seven Hundred Piglets

The late winter sunlight streamed through the musty velvet curtains and stretched across the wide pine floorboards. Clifford Pyncheon leaned forward across his desk, almost pressing his nose against the large computer screen in anticipation. He began to count down.

"Ten, nine, eight, seven ..."

His sister Hepzibah burst into the room.

"Oh, not again Clifford!" she shouted.

"Six, five, four ..."

"You promised!" She threw her dishtowel at his head, but he barely noticed.

"Three, two, one ..."

"Phoebe, get in here! He's at it again!" Hepzibah yelled.

But it was too late. There was nothing his sister or Phoebe could do. The bidding was complete.

"I won! I won!" He jumped from his chair and skipped across the room.

The Salem townsfolk all gossiped about the cheerful change in Clifford since young Phoebe had come to live at Pyncheon House. And it was true that Clifford's formerly sullen, haunted, crotchety demeanor had shifted into something resembling cheerfulness. Their old house, with its foreboding seven gables and dusty furniture, had become less oppressive as Clifford bustled about during the day, dusting and rearranging furniture into a more pleasing formation.

But the three of them knew it had nothing to do with Phoebe living there.

Several months before, worried about Clifford's despondent state, Phoebe had introduced him to the wonderful world of eBay. His eyes lit up as he began to peruse hundreds of collectibles from across the globe. He marveled at antique china from the Orient. He drooled over guns from India. But when he stumbled upon a seller advertising an antique cookie jar, he lost his head.

"Just look at him, isn't he cute?" Clifford had teared up as he stared at the picture. "He looks just like the one Mum had when I was a boy. I must buy it."

It wasn't just any cookie jar. It was a piglet cookie jar. And thus began Clifford's obsession. He immediately entered into a two-day bidding war with a woman named Agnes whose picture profile showed a smiling kitten.

"She's no kitten," Clifford had muttered as she continually bid higher for the eerie, ceramic piece. "She's the devil."

But in the end he'd triumphed. He won his first piglet. Little did Hepzibah or Phoebe know, but Clifford was about to take on the obsessed existence of a true collector. Or in his case, a piglet cookie jar collector. He'd stalked eBay. He talked Hepzibah into traveling far and wide to the surrounding towns, searching for estate sales and antiques shops for his beloved piglets.

Hepzibah glared at her brother as he continued his victory dance around the living room. Carpenters had built shelves into the kitchen and dining room to house his piglets. Extra storage bins were placed in the cellar after all the shelves filled to capacity.

"You do realize we have no more room." She gritted her teeth.

"But sister!" Clifford stopped in his tracks. "Don't you realize? This was number seven hundred. This little piglet has joined a happy family of seven hundred cookie jars from all over the globe!"

Phoebe wrung her hands, glancing back and forth between her relatives. She'd already had to get rid of most of her belongings to store piglets in her bedroom wardrobe.

"That's it Clifford. I'm cutting you off. No more collecting."

He froze like a deer in the path of an oncoming Mack truck.

"You wouldn't."

"I most certainly would. I'm canceling your PayPal account. Your obsession has far surpassed normalcy. It's a sickness. Of course we've been pleased to see you perk up and shed your former depression, but it's time to get a grip."

Clifford sunk into a nearby chair, taking in the nearby dining room where an entire wall of piglet cookie jars smiled at him.

"But . . . but . . . I love them."

"Don't be silly! It's just stuff! Stuff I tell you! You can't take any of this with you! It's just collecting dust. Or in your case, it's seven hundred pig cookie jars collecting dust."

Clifford sniffed forlornly as Hepzibah marched out of the room.

Phoebe put her arm around Clifford. "There, there. I'm sure we can find something else to interest you. And just look around, you have so many cookie jars to comfort you, surely you don't need to go on collecting?"

Clifford sniffed and wiped his nose with his sleeve. "Well, I've heard there's a man outside Salem who sells handmade wind chimes. I do love those. Maybe I could collect those instead?"

Phoebe paused, unsure of how the conversation had shifted from ceramic piglets to wind chimes. She pondered the noise level seven hundred chimes might make swinging from the backyard trees and choked a little.

"Yes, that sounds interesting after all." Clifford smiled widely, patting Phoebe on the hand. "You know what they say, once a collector, always a collector!"

She watched him bound from the room with enthusiasm. She thought of the quiet, depressed man he'd been when she'd moved in. A man who had never typed on a keyboard. A man unaware of eBay's existence. A man without a single solitary piglet cookie jar. She rose and looked out the window as Clifford examined the lower tree branches near the back terrace, mentally arranging his future collection.

Phoebe crossed her arms. "Of all the half cousins and relatives I could have chosen to live with, I had to pick the nut jobs. I wonder if it's too late for me to move in with Aunt Hattie? She only has ten cats. That's really not so bad . . ."

"Lay one finger on that mink stole and I'll stab you with these cocktail skewers."

A small elderly woman leaned forward menacingly, the glow of the overhead chandelier reflecting off her lavender-tinted hair. She clutched a set of Scottie dog cocktail skewers in her age-spotted hands, ready to go to fisticuffs.

The offending party, a petite middle-aged woman with perfectly coifed blonde hair and wearing a pink sweater set pursed her overly glossed lips and stepped closer to the mink stole laying on a nearby folding table. "Back off, lady, I saw it first."

My eyes widened and I sucked in my breath as I eavesdropped, gripping my prize McCoy vase tightly lest anyone tackle me for it. I glanced across the room at Angela. Her eyes were wide and unblinking.

A nearby businesswoman in a gray suit muttered, "That's no way to talk to a grandmother."

But I wasn't fooled. Grandma was holding one skewer like a shiv.

Quickly noticing she had an audience, Grandma switched tactics and played the sympathy card. "My husband always wanted to be able to buy me a mink stole; we just never had enough money. Estate sale prices are the only thing I can afford now on my fixed income."

Pink Sweater Set's eyes narrowed suspiciously as she checked out the $40 price tag. "I'm very sorry dear, but I already planned to buy it. My daughter's always wanted one."

I kept an eye on Grandma's cocktail skewers warily and exchanged another nervous glance with Angela. The afternoon light outside dimmed as a cloud passed over, long shadows creeping across the room in octopus tentacles of foreboding.

We'd seen this before. It's what we regulars refer to as an Estate Sale Face-off. It's similar to a fashion walk-off, except most of the participants need hip replacements, and instead of strutting in heels the two teams use vintage golf clubs and brass fire tongs as weapons.

Grandma shifted her feet, her support hose stretching. The wheels behind her gray eyes were turning, debating whether to stab or tackle.

The businesswoman next to me, holding a large box of Pyrex, stepped forward to try her hand at peacemaking. "Listen, there must be some way to reconcile the situation."

Pink Sweater Set gave a bitter laugh. "Listen lady, I came here today in search of two things: a mink stole and vintage Pyrex for my daughter's Christmas present. And since you've obviously scarfed up the entire box of Pyrex, I'm not about to let Granny Chicken here run off with the stole."

Another onlooker elbowed me. "Oooh . . . now this is getting good."

"Well!" Business Suit hugged her box of goods tighter. "I'm sorry, but it just so happens that I'm a Pyrex collector."

"See! It's not so fun when the shoe's on the other foot!" Pink Sweater Set clutched the mink and the three women stood in an odd circle, a veritable Estate Sale O.K. Corral.

I stealthily shifted the McCoy in my hand, hiding it behind my back, and signaled to Angela. We slunk away from the oncoming train wreck. Call me a coward, but once you've been subpoenaed for an estate sale brawl, you never make the same mistake twice. My thrift-shopping mantra has become, "Hear no evil, see no evil."

We ventured into the next room, the auditory remnants of the fight fading behind us.

"Can you believe that? Collectors are a shockingly obsessed group of people," Angela whispered. She clutched a stack of vintage fabric tightly, lest anyone run over screaming, "Mine! All Mine!" and jerk it from her hands.

It was Saturday and Angela and I were shopping. While most women congregated at the local TJ Maxx and had lunch at Olive Garden, Angela and I preferred to visit the local estate sales and eat grilled cheese at Sonic.

We found ourselves in a dining room time-warped from the early 1960s: gray-and-aqua flocked wallpaper, midcentury furniture beneath a crystal chandelier, and a complete set of atomic star pattern china strewn about for the taking. Next to the drape-and-sheer covered picture window hung an assortment of party dresses, reminiscent of Jackie Kennedy. I walked past, letting my hand brush the nubby silks and chiffons as Grandma yelped in the distance, "There's no respect for the elderly anymore!"

It was a confusing parallel. There we were, veritable vultures in dress slacks, calculating our way around someone's private home. The ranting of a ridiculous fight rang in our ears when we were, in fact, profiting from an occurrence that should have been sacred. Hushed. Perhaps even mourned.

I glanced at the top of the dining room buffet table, noted a small water ring near the edge, and felt my throat catch. I eyed it for a moment, realizing that the woman who had lived and died in this home, the woman who had worn her party dresses to the club and treasured her pink Pyrex set, was now gone.

Angela picked up a well-worn copy of *Sense and Sensibility* from the bookshelf. "You should buy this. After all, you Dashwood girls need several copies."

I grinned, befuddled as always at her comparisons of my family to Austen's illustrious Dashwoods. There was a tremendous amount of irony in likening three ladylike, literary sisters to three unladylike, Southern sisters whose vocabularies were rife with idioms like, *"Don't you dare pee on me and tell me it's raining!"*

I returned my thoughts to the room around me, to the woman who, I imagined, had walked through these rooms every morning wearing slippers and carrying a cup of coffee.

She had spent mornings in her pine-paneled TV room watching the news as her children boarded a school bus on the curb out front. She had placed freshly cut zinnias from the backyard garden in the McCoy vase I held in my hand. She and her husband had hosted dinner parties and holiday meals—complete with Scottie dog cocktail skewers—in the very dining room I was standing in. Perhaps a guest caused the water ring on the buffet table when they forgot to use a coaster.

As we wound our way into the kitchen, a cheerful room with white cabinets and bright yellow Formica countertops, I realized this woman and I might have been friends. I might have been a neighbor who drank coffee in the built-in breakfast nook and watched her bake a cake. We might have commiserated about hollyhock seeds that refused to bloom, or the new neighbor who left his garbage cans out all week.

I hung a left and made my way through the entry hall, its walls embossed in a red-and-white Dutch-style pattern, as the cuckoo clock over the entry table chimed, perhaps for the last time in this house. And it was then that I was overwhelmed with the sudden knowledge that my house might someday be subject to an estate sale and pillaged.

Someday my grandmother's Homer Laughlin Orange Tree bowls would be fodder for a skirmish. Obsessed collectors, total strangers, might stand in my dining room and think the same thoughts, wondering about my dresses, my dishes, my furniture. My life.

I sniffed loudly, hoping Angela wouldn't notice as I wiped the moisture from my eyes.

Angela smiled a little as we passed the formal living room again, its spring green carpet matted with age, its retro ivory-upholstered furniture bearing witness to the mink stole/Pyrex dispute still taking place. I noticed the moisture in her eyes too.

It was probably not the best choice for a Saturday outing.

The Friday before, Good Friday ironically enough, the doctors detected more tumors in the lining of Angela's lungs.

Those doctors who in the beginning had encouraged her to "think positive and consider yourself cancer-free" were now declaring her cancer-ridden. It meant more chemo, more surgeries, more fear. In her words, "Tumor Fred left Fredlettes."

She'd called to tell me the night before, her voice strained and tired. And then she'd said the unthinkable.

"Liz, I'm thinking of making a list of my possessions. I think I'm going to specify who should have what, in case, well, you know. If I die."

At the time I bit my tongue and said nothing, because I really wanted to shout, "Shut up! I don't want to think about this!!"

"I really want my sister to have some specific things, and my little niece Evelyn."

I didn't respond.

"I know you don't like to talk about these things. But is there anything you'd like to have? From me?"

My brain began to spin at the calmness in her voice, at her strength of mind to even be able to consider such things.

"You're not going to die," I said, trying my best to keep my voice level over the phone.

"We're all going to die eventually," she laughed slightly, "and I'm pretty sure the ones we leave behind will appreciate a little instruction on the matter of our belongings."

"But you're not dying today, so let's not talk about it," I insisted.

I could almost hear her smile over the phone. "Fine, have it your way. But I'm still making a list."

We'd hung up, but not before agreeing that a girls' day of estate sale shopping was in order. But as we stood there, in that old house, watching the women around us flutter over a dead woman's belongings like meat-picking vultures, I realized it was a painfully close subject for Angela.

"Let's get out of here," I stated a little too loudly. "Let's go watch that new movie, *Miss Pettigrew Lives for a Day*."

"That sounds delightful. I've been wanting to see it," she said softly. Then she leaned closer, smiling. "See what I mean? If this woman had made a list, she'd have saved everyone a lot of trouble."

I shot Angela a stern look. I didn't want to discuss it.

She patted my arm. "You can't fight everything all the time Liz."

As we made our way through the crowds to the front of the house, I realized that the woman who had once lived here, who had once laid claim to a home and belongings and clothes, had moved on. She had moved on to a better place, a wonderful place with its own glorious versions of Pyrex nesting bowls and midcentury consoles. I thought that if given the chance, she wouldn't come back for all this. And that if she were high above looking down and watching Grandma and Pink Sweater Set host a tug-o-war in her living room, she would chuckle, poke the angel standing next to her, and say, "Take a look at these goobers!"

I took a deep breath, passing the turquoise-and-pink master bedroom as I handed a worker my cash and exited with my new McCoy vase. I knew that I would never forget the house I bought it in, or my version of the woman who owned it. Possessions, as much as we love and fight and scrap for them, are only a symbol of the inner workings of our minds and hearts. Our homes, our sunlit dining rooms, white-tiled kitchens, and brushed McCoy collections are not what make us, well, us. They just serve to represent our tastes, our home lives, our quirky inner workings that tick to their own unique beat.

I knew one day I would leave my little McCoy vase to another generation of eager hands, just as one day Angela would leave a piece of jewelry to her sister, or a broach to her niece. We didn't know when it would happen, or how it would happen, or where it would happen, but whether we have cancer or heart problems, or simply die of old age, we all leave our belongings eventually. My McCoy vase will move from my white-painted cottage-style kitchen to another shelf, in another house, in another town. And that is okay. That is how it's meant to be. And perhaps someone, whoever buys it, will wonder about me.

As Angela and I situated our goods in the backseat of my car, we glanced up in time to see Grandma exiting the house.

"Well, will you look at that?" Angela pointed.

The old lady was moving slowly, maneuvering her walker down the cracked sidewalk in the direction of a large mustard-hued Cadillac. Swinging from her walker was a bag stuffed with skewers and . . . a mink stole.

I couldn't help but grin as I got into my car, and I thought, for just a second, that I heard a woman's laughter overhead.

CHAPTER 12

Sleepwalker, I Married Him

"Eddie!" Jane Eyre-Rochester *hissed into the darkness, rolling onto her side and aggressively adjusting her pillow.* "You're snoring again."

She was answered with a resounding snort, and then Edward Rochester's snoring fell back into its cadence of peaks and valleys, snorts and grunts. They reverberated off the plaster walls, high into the rafters. Jane pursed her lips, feeling every inclination to sleep fall away, replaced by white hot rage. She looked around the room, trying to distract herself by admiring the carefully crafted crown molding overhead and the built-in bookshelves by the stained glass window. But it was no use.

They'd all warned her.

"Don't marry him! Marry that nice St. John boy instead. Edward Rochester has already been married once, and you know how that turned out. He will only cause you trouble."

But she hadn't listened.

Honestly, Jane didn't mind Edward's dark and brooding nature. She didn't mind his smelly socks or daily refusals to comb his hair properly. She'd accepted his permanent scowl and his inability to lose gracefully at cards.

But this blasted snoring. No one had warned her about this.

She exhaled deeply and rolled on her side away from him and shut her eyes tightly. She would fall asleep. She would will it to happen.

However, as soon as she had counted five fluffy sheep, Edward's snoring changed rhythm, becoming louder and more interspersed with gurgling.

"That's it!" She threw the covers back.

It had been four days since she'd slept an entire night. Three days since she'd smiled. Two days since she'd bathed, and one day since she'd allowed Edward to kiss her.

Jane once again gazed around the room, her sleep-deprived, puffy, red-rimmed eyes examining the red velvet drapes, the heavy oriental carpets, the carefully chosen mahogany furniture. After Edward rebuilt a more modest version of Thornfield Hall, she had spent months consulting with interior decorators and perusing magazines for decorating inspiration. She had agonized over feather pillows, duvet covers, quilts, and elegant French-style furniture. She wanted to decorate in a style completely opposite of Eddie's first wife. There would be no purple shag carpeting or hideous psychedelic light fixtures in the new Thornfield Hall.

But no matter how beautiful the room, no matter how much effort she'd put into constructing the perfect bedchamber, it meant nothing to her now. Only blissful sleep mattered.

Edward snorted again, twisting sideways and yanking the covers.

She'd heard tales of new mothers so sleep-deprived and bewildered by their screaming babies that they ran through the streets after dark yelling, "Somebody help me! A strange man keeps calling me his wife and all these kids call me Mommy! I don't know any of them, it's a trap! It's a hoax! It's a conspiracy I tell you!"

But until this moment she'd doubted the importance of sleep in her own life. She often bragged that after a mere six hours of sleep she could can vegetables, balance the budget, instruct the maids, walk five miles, and mend her dresses. She had proclaimed that even on five hours of sleep there were no shadows beneath her eyes, no scowl on her face.

But right now, as she gazed down at her beloved Eddie, his mouth slack and open, a tiny stream of drool gracing his cheek, the cruel, cold, insane hand of sleep deprivation overtook her brain. Her thoughts turned once again to his first wife. Had she been insane and obsessed with fire? Yes. But what drove her there? How did she become the wild-haired, crazy-eyed woman who roamed hallways late at night, unable to sleep?

Jane listened to another resounding snore rip past her husband's lips and began to rethink her predecessor's insanity. Perhaps Wife Number One burned the house down just to get some sleep.

Jane's arm began to lift as if phantom muscles were controlling it. Her hand stretched out toward Edward's face, his boar-hog snores still blasting past his reverberating lips.

"Must . . . get . . . sleep . . ." she mumbled as she pinched Edward's nostrils closed. With her other hand she jammed his mouth shut.

For a few merciful seconds she remembered what a silent bedchamber was like. Somewhere in the distance a mockingbird chirped. The clock in the hallway ticked softly. The moonlight created beautiful spiderweb patterns on the plush carpeting. It was a silent, peaceful heaven.

It was heaven, that is, until Edward's oxygen-deprived brain woke him up.

His arms flailed and his eyes shot open, wide and terrified. His pupils focused on her face, noting her assassin hands. Begrudgingly, she released him.

"You . . ." he gasped, hand to throat, finger pointing. "You tried to kill me!"

"Don't be overly dramatic. I just wanted some peace and quiet!"

"You tried to kill me!" He jumped up, tripping on the twisted bedding.

She shrugged. "I would have let go eventually."

But deep down, Jane felt remorse. After all, poor Edward was understandably sensitive about the whole wife-killing-her-husband scenario.

"Eventually? When? After I was dead?" Edward's face paled as he studied his bride in horror.

"No, I didn't want to kill you. I just wanted you to be quiet!" Jane jumped from bed and rounded the footboard. "Do you *have any idea what it's like lying next to you? Night after night with your constant wood-saw snoring, your dead-fish gurgles, your wallowing-pig snorts?"*

Edward's bottom lip began to protrude. Despite his bluster, his delicate feelings were quite easily bruised.

"Look, I'm sorry. But if I don't get some sleep, I'm going to do something crazy," Jane said.

Edward blinked, "Would it help if I slept in the other room tonight?"

"Yes," she smiled sweetly, "that would help immensely."

"Okay then," he mumbled, gathering his pillows and trudging from the room.

Jane snuggled into the center of the bed, her muscles relaxing for the first time in days. Finally, she would sleep the slumber of babes. No more counting sheep, no more wishing her husband was dead.

And somewhere down the hall, within the darkness, Edward fearfully snapped the guest room door lock.

"I'll miss you."

I eyed Matt suspiciously. He's a man of great demonstrative affection. He fills my car up with gas every week so I don't have to. He buys bags of Peppermint Patties and puts them in the fridge because he knows I like them cold. I know he loves me because he checks the air in my tires and holds my hand in church. But when it comes to words, he's not exactly a verbal Don Juan.

"I'll be back early, probably six or seven tomorrow morning," I said.

I threw a clean pair of socks and a sweatshirt into my backpack while he watched.

"I'm glad you're going. But I sleep better when you're here. It gets lonely."

I glanced at him again in alarm. These statements were the Matt equivalent of a love fest. I hugged him, assuring him I'd be home at dawn.

The evening light dimmed as I put my backpack in the car. The summer air was stifling, a combination of an entire day's worth of sunshine and humidity. I flipped the car air conditioner to full blast and headed to the hospital to spend the night with Angela.

A few weeks had passed since our estate sale outing. She faced another lung tumor, another incision, and more unanswered questions. I'd lost count of the surgeries during the last year. As the days passed she grew quiet, the silent wheels in her brain turning. I could see she was sick of it. I spent a lot of time examining her face. I worried about the undercurrents I saw swirling beneath her everyday conversations about politics and hospital food. Every now and then I thought I saw a hint of resignation in her eyes. That scared me more than her cancer.

I started my car, pondering Matt's statement. He didn't sleep well when I was gone. The irony was, for the longest time, I couldn't sleep with him around.

As a newlywed, I envisioned certain aspects of domestic life in very definite ways. I saw us eating breakfast together on a vintage cloth–covered table. Never happened. Mostly because I have always risen and left the house before Matt cracks an eyelid. I envisioned us curled up together on the couch, watching movies, holding hands, sharing a bowl of popcorn. In reality, I hog the couch and push Matt onto the floor where he stretches out on every pillow in the house. We've also discovered that we don't share food very well.

I also daydreamed about the perfect bedroom, a romantic retreat with wispy curtains, fluffy bedding, painted furniture, and candles. I planned a color palette of seaside colors: greens and aqua and grays. I built it up in my mind, a perfect retreat for REM perfection. And better yet, never having to sleep alone again. I'm talking about the ultimate girlish daydream: cuddling. Going to sleep together, feet touching, having someone to hug during a late night thunderstorm. I saw myself waking up, rolling over, and smiling contentedly into Matt's face as the early morning sunlight shone through gauzy curtains and onto the ocean-hued room around us.

This did not go as planned.

Our first bedroom didn't exactly mesh with my dreams, especially since our rental house walls couldn't be painted and had heavy wood trim. I made a concession, choosing soothing neutral beige bedding, white curtains, and black-and-white prints for the wall. Ultimate seaside retreat it was not, but it was peaceful and put together. I was satisfied and ready for romantic cuddling to commence, followed by hours of blissful sleep.

My first hint that something might go awry happened on our honeymoon. We were in our hotel suite, and I was half awake thinking how lovely it was that I'd married a man who didn't snore.

Suddenly Matt sat up, turned to me with a dreamy smile and half-closed eyelids, and said, "Would you please tell the spaceman to stop wearing my socks?"

"Excuse me?" I clutched the bedcovers to my chin, alarmed.

Matt's gaze turned toward the ceiling and he shook his fist at what I assumed to be the spaceman. "I don't have time to take a trip to the moon!"

Before I could respond, Matt rolled back over and continued to sleep. I later mentioned this to his mother, who laughed.

"Oh yes, Matt has been known to sleepwalk. When he was a little boy he came downstairs one night, ate a Popsicle, and had an entire conversation with me while he was sleeping. It was so cute."

I smiled and agreed. Eating Popsicles and talking about spacemen *was* pretty adorable.

But the events that followed were decidedly less amusing. My first encounter with "sleeping with the enemy" happened several months later. I awoke suddenly in the middle of the night, one eye wide and unblinking into the darkness of our bedroom. But after a few moments of complete confusion and disorientation, I realized my right eye was wide and unblinking because Matt was leaning over me, peeling my eyelid back with his finger, his other finger poking my eyeball like a demented ophthalmologist.

I screamed. And then I punched him in the jaw.

It was a confused scene. I flailed wildly, throwing bedcovers everywhere in dazed horror. Matt, whose eyes immediately shifted from the glazed state of a sleepwalker to complete consciousness when my fist made impact with his face, clutched his injured jaw and repeated over and over, "You hit me. You hit me."

"*Why would you do that?*" I shrieked.

"Do what?" Matt's face was blanched with confusion and panic.

"You were . . . you were . . . poking my eye!" I rubbed my injured optical cavity with righteous indignation.

"No, I didn't! I woke up when you hit me!"

And that's when the cold bath of reality swept over me. My sweet beloved was, as it turned out, a notorious sleepwalker. And while I still loved this good-hearted man with rabid devotion, I began to worry. Seriously worry. Was there a possibility that he was a dangerous sleeper? Was he Jekyll and Hyde? A nice man by day with a subconscious eye-poking alter ego by night?

As the sky grew dark in the evenings, I was not comforted by our carefully decorated bedroom. Instead I watched him suspiciously. I also purchased a black velvet sleeping mask to protect my precious vision. If things got worse, I was resigned to buying sports goggles.

Weeks passed without incident. I stopped contemplating separate bedrooms with locks and let my guard down. And that's when the second altercation transpired.

It was a Friday night; cool fall air blew through our open windows as we stayed up late watching a movie. It was around one in the morning when I drifted off to sleep, and it was a mere three hours later that I awoke in utter panic.

The entire room seemed to be rocking, and I had one thought: earthquake. My mind began to race. I had to wake Matt. We had to grab Mabel and get out of the house. But it was no earthquake at all.

It was Matt, gripping the back of my underwear with his fist and jerking as hard as he could. Lest anyone think this story is about to get raunchy, let me assure you, it is not. You see, I was on the receiving end of what people like to refer to as a "wedgie." And not just any schoolyard prank wedgie with a joking yank at the top of my underwear. Matt was clutching a fistful of my undergarments and yanking upward with the strength of ten men.

I swung my elbow backward as hard as I could, kicking my legs and flailing like a fish on the end of a hook. Once again, we went through the same scenario.

"*What are you doing?*"

Matt released his vice grip on my now decimated underpants and lay there blinking, stunned from slumber. "Huh?"

I jumped from bed, adjusting my stretched out underwear with as much dignity as I could muster. "You were doing it again!"

"Did I do something in my sleep?"

This time he sat upright, nervously checking to make sure I still had both my eyes.

"*Yes!*" I snapped. "Only this time you were giving me a *wedgie.*"

Silence hung between us with the crackling intensity of an electric storm. And then Matt made a critical mistake. He laughed.

"A wedgie, huh? That's kind of funny," he chuckled.

"Really?" I screeched. "You only say that because you weren't the one being assaulted."

"It's not as bad as last time." He grinned sleepily.

I looked at him with the anger of one hundred violent felons. "Find somewhere else to sleep."

And so poor, pitiful, eye-poking, wedgie-giving, misunderstood Matt gathered his pillow and trudged down the hall to the guest room.

I lay back down, looking around my dimly lit bedroom of horrors, unable to be comforted by its carefully planned decor. Who cared if our duvet cover matched the sheets? Who cared if the lavender candles on the dresser were spa-like? I was faced with a giant conundrum: Did I continue slumbering next to my sweet but nocturnally frightening husband? Or, did we go the Victorian route and opt for separate bedrooms less than six months after reciting our vows?

After all, if I had my own bedroom I could redecorate again.

I decided to stick it out and eventually the problem resolved itself. How? I'm not sure. A doctor attributed these incidents to stress. We were college students. Matt worked full time, I held down two jobs, and we were newly married. It was a veritable stress-o-rama. But as we got into the groove, Matt's sleep improved. The nighttime mutterings and hall pacing slowed down.

Once, and only once, did Matt mistake the corner of our bedroom for a toilet. There is nothing more jarring than being awoken by the sound of urine splattering onto shag carpeting. But barring that ordeal, sleep time has been peaceful. The bedroom has been redecorated numerous times and is now swathed in soothing seaside shades. Cuddling has commenced. And when it's cold at night, Matt lets me stick my cold toes on his warm feet.

But every now and then, as we're drifting off to sleep, I reach for my sleeping mask. Just to be on the safe side.

I parked my car and entered the hospital. Night-shift workers also headed inside, as beleaguered day workers marched into the parking lot in droves. Hospitals take on a different vibe at night. All the noise of appointments, doctor pages, lunch carts, and general bustle slows down. The lights in the rooms go out. The night staff make quiet jokes and struggle to stay awake.

In the daytime hospital you can distract yourself. But in the night-shift hospital, it's hard to think of anything else besides sickness. As I walked through Angela's wing, I passed by dozens of dark doorways. Blue TVs illuminated the faces of people who were lonely, scared, and hurting. You can ignore those things when the sun is shining and the corridors are packed with people, but when it's just your lonely footsteps in the hallway, there's no avoiding it. Hospitals are sad places where no one sleeps peacefully.

Angela's room was dark. The TV was off. There were dozens of tubes and blinking lights and the peaceful hum of the fan beside her bed.

"Ang?" I whispered. She didn't stir. The night nurse had already visited with her tray full of drugs and sedatives. Truthfully, I was glad Angela was out. I hoped that she'd pass through the night oblivious and awake to the beautiful pink dawn.

There were several women who volunteered to spend the night with Angela at the hospital, and it was my turn. Bryan spent every day at the hospital, while working the night shift the rest of the time. It was a daunting schedule, and we hoped that by staying with her at night, he might worry less. Her sister Anna and I had started to talk weekly by phone. It grieved her to be so far away while Angela was hurting, but there was nothing that could be done.

I carefully arranged my pillow and bag, settling into the reclining chair by her bed. It wasn't comfortable. But then again, I wasn't there to get good sleep. I was there to keep her from being alone, from waking up to an empty room. To sit and wait.

I dozed off but woke up rigid, completely afraid to move. The room was black, blacker than usual. Angela's oxygen monitor sounded its beep regularly, but I knew that wasn't what woke me. I wasn't sure what it was, I only knew that pure, muscle-freezing horror had overtaken me.

The room was dark; I could barely see the blinking lights from Angela's IV and the equipment beside her bed. I lay there, stricken with terror. I thought cancer itself had filled the room. It crept through the air ducts and wafted under the door, filling the room with its black, choking smoke. It felt utterly evil.

I tried to move, to whisper Angela's name, but nothing happened. My hands tingled, paralyzed. Cold sweat broke across my forehead and for the first time in my life I was truly, totally afraid.

There was nothing to do but pray. For some that might seem a desperate, weak knee-jerk reaction by someone steeped in religion as a child. Some would say I was having a very serious panic attack. But as I lay there amid the most evil presence I'd ever known, there was no other option.

"God, please protect us."

This is what came to me. I whispered it silently over and over. I'm not sure how much time passed, but all at once the horrible feelings stopped. The roar in my ears ceased and I could move again.

I sat up, leaning over to check on Angela. She slumbered peacefully—unaware of whatever had transpired. I was thankful the horrible insanity had been confined to me only. The clock on my cell phone read 3:30 a.m.

I rose, donning my sneakers and shoving my hair into a bun. I needed to get out of that room. I needed air.

Waving to the nurses, I helped myself to a Coke in the family break room and headed outside. The front of the hospital was deserted, a stoplight blinking in the distance. The moon was huge and bright overhead, the summer air stagnant and humid. I slumped onto a park bench, weak with relief that whatever had just happened was over. And then I began to think about God.

Despite my promises to pray for Angela, my relationship with God Almighty had continued to be one of polite disconnect. I figured that if I didn't bother him, he wouldn't bother me. We were like the stereotypical husband and wife, each seated at either end of a long dining room table in a vast formal dining room. There were twenty empty seats between us, a large chandelier overhead, gilded mirrors lining the walls, and fresh flowers blocking our view of one another. Every so often I might peer around and say, "Pass the salt?" and God would motion to one of the servants in the shadows to deliver the shaker to me. That was the extent of our relationship.

On that night, huddled pathetically in front of the hospital, I got up from the metaphorical table. I stomped my way past mirrors and flower arrangements, alarming the servants, and slammed my plate down, pulled out a chair, and sat down at God's elbow.

I realize most people would be horrified to witness what happened outside that hospital. They would wisely duck and look upward, expecting lightning to blast me into a singed spot on the ground as I stood beneath the hospital security lights, raised my fist, and began to yell.

But God sent no lightning. He cut me some slack.

"God, what the hell? I don't understand it! I don't understand any of it!"

I glanced from side to side. After all, it was a hospital where surely there existed a ward full of people who talked to God and got the privilege of a forty-eight-hour lockup. This was behavior definitely unfitting for my literary heroes. Jo March would never use the H-word at God. Even my fiery Anne would have balked at raising her fist to the heavens, wisely casting her eyes downward. But seeing no onlookers, I continued.

"Are you even there? Can you even hear me? Enough! It's enough! She has more than she can bear!"

I paused to catch my breath and railed on.

"Aren't you capable of sending angels to save her? Where are they? Where are you?"

I felt the tears sliding down my cheeks. I knew I'd had a full-on panic attack. I knew if I didn't stop yelling, a nice doctor would lock me in a padded room. And it was there, while I stood and mascara slid down my face in Alice Cooper-esque streaks, that I heard God.

"Elizabeth, do you love me?"

The air caught in my throat and I choked a little. This was it. The big one. My complete psychotic break. Any second I would begin to drool and run circles around the landscaping. I breathed very deeply, and I heard the voice again. It was very, very kind.

"Then be grateful."

Now, I'd heard about people who had conversations with God. They were mainly relegated to fantastical vacation Bible school stories about pillars of flame and arks full of animals. But there was no pillar of flame in that parking lot. It was a voice in my head. It was not me.

I was taken aback for two reasons.

1. Voices in your head never bode well. Just look at Joan of Arc.

2. This voice, God, was telling me to be grateful. Grateful for what? My dying friend? Her mental anguish? My personal breakdown?

I turned swiftly and marched back inside the hospital, thereby ending my first two-way conversation with God. I, like Scarlett, would think about it another day. There are times when we go weeks, months, even years with seemingly no communication or interaction with the divine. And when it happens in such a rush, when suddenly not only are you praying as you've never prayed before, but God speaks to you . . . it's as shocking as taking an arctic plunge.

When the sun rose, I was sitting up in the chair by Angela's bed. I watched her open her eyes and give me a half smile. She was weak and it was all she could manage.

"Good morning," she said.

"Morning," I said.

The minute we made eye contact I realized I would never tell her about what had happened. I never wanted her to know how afraid I'd been with her, for her, in that very room. Would it have comforted me to share my experience of paralyzing fear? Yes. She would have no doubt presented several reasonable arguments and ideas about what it could have been. She also would have offered me a few of her "happy pills" had I told her that God spoke to me.

But as much as I wanted to treat her normally, I didn't want her to be afraid, because the overwhelming fear that had hijacked my sense of reason the night before wasn't for me. It was for her. It was for the unknown and the horrible things she might still face.

C. S. Lewis once said, "We are what we believe we are." Angela needed to believe she was whole and would be well again. She didn't need to believe in scary, cancerous shadows that could fill a room and reduce her friend to hysterics.

"Go home, get some sleep," she said as she sat upright, adjusting her bed. "You look terrible. Swing by a drive-through and get a breakfast burrito, that always seems to cheer you up."

I hugged her briefly and gathered my bag. I knew that if I didn't leave soon, I would start crying.

"Love you," I said as I walked quickly from the room.

"Love you too," she called after me.

I drove home and parked in the driveway. I sat in my car, listening to the mockingbirds in the trees. I was confused. I was exhausted. But somehow, I felt more at peace than I could ever remember. The tightness in my chest, the numbness in my hands, the tension in my neck: They were gone.

I went inside and crawled into bed with Matt. Our blue bedroom was dark and cool. He was still sleeping, snoring loudly. I reached out and put my arms around him, an unfamiliar feeling of calm washing over me.

Matt rolled over suddenly and propped himself up on one elbow.

His eyes were half open, and I recognized that "face" immediately. He was still asleep.

"Ugh, not again Matt. I cannot handle this right now." I pulled a pillow over my face.

"So, let me get this straight . . ." He smirked, his eyes glazed over.

"Matt . . . wake up," I muttered, irritated at the thought of getting my underwear yanked.

"Wait, wait. Wait just a minute. So you're trying to tell me you don't like *Star Wars?*"

Apparently he was in the middle of a dream-argument with me. And even in a state of sleep, Matt was offended that I might not deeply care for the original George Lucas trilogy.

I pushed his shoulder. "Matt, wake up. You're talking in your sleep again, and of course I like *Star Wars*."

He exhaled loudly, plunking his head back onto the pillow. I couldn't help but smile at his slack-jawed face, the massive snores erupting once again from his open mouth. I moved closer, placing my head on his chest and closing my eyes.

How could I be grateful when my friend was so sick? I didn't have the foggiest idea what God was talking about. But I was, for the first time in my life, on God's end of the dining table. I was praying, and apparently, he was listening after all.

And even though Matt's snores ruffled my hair, I smiled, thankful he was there. In no time at all, I was snoring too.

Chapter 13

The Not-So-Great Cookie

"Now Tom, there are a few things we need to discuss." Mrs. Buchanan's plump pink face was uncharacteristically stern as she carefully added sugar to his coffee.

"Sure, Mom, what's up?" Tom smiled at his kindly mother, appreciating the way she buttered his toast just right as the sun streamed through the windows, brightening the spotless kitchen.

She set his breakfast plate before him, reaching back to pluck his favorite jelly from the refrigerator. "We need to talk about Daisy."

A shadow passed over Tom's face. As if the stock market crash, subsequent Great Depression, and the loss of his company hadn't been enough; there was also the memory of the whole Daisy and Gatsby debacle that followed behind him like a great cloud of guilt.

Mrs. Buchanan continued. "That Daisy, she's certainly transformed into a whirlwind of energy, that's for sure. But I wanted to talk to you about your husbandly duties."

Tom crossed his arms, suddenly not hungry for the buttered toast and grits on his plate. His stomach did a somersault as he pushed his chair away from the table, readying himself to bolt from the room. His father had long ago given him the "birds and bees" speech and the thought of his gray-haired mother (who could only bring herself to spell the words "p-o-o p-o-o" in hushed whispers) schooling him on bedroom etiquette was too much for his brain to process.

"Whoa, Mom. Just whoa. I don't want to talk about this with you."

Mrs. Buchanan eyed her twitchy son, puzzled at his ashen face and dry heaves. "Sweetheart, I wanted to talk to you about Daisy's cooking abilities."

"Oh, is that all?" Tom wiped the cold sweat from his forehead in relief.

"Yes. Now, I've raised you a certain way, dear. You grew up with cooks and pastry chefs at your every command. They knew how to sweeten your coffee and bake your favorite cookies every Friday. But I'm noticing how thin you've become lately. Is everything all right?"

Tom slumped in his chair, gazing around his mother's huge, well-maintained kitchen with white granite countertops and professional grade cookware. Ever since the Great Crash, ever since he and Daisy lost all their money and the mansion in West Egg, things had been going downhill. He found himself listless and drifting. On the other hand, Daisy was thriving. She had transformed from vapid flapper to businesswoman in a matter of months.

"Daisy is pretty busy with her job. The good news is Daisy's Donuts are selling by the truckload. The bad news is, well, she's not home to cook for me and we're not in a position to hire any help at the moment."

Mrs. Buchanan distractedly folded a hand-embroidered dish towel. "Well, son, the fact of the matter is, the good old days are gone. The only reason your father and I didn't lose our house is because of the loan Uncle Filton gave us. The bottom line is, Daisy's probably not going to take the time to cut the crust off your peanut-butter-and-honey sandwiches every morning when she's packing up your mid-afternoon snack."

Tom frowned. It was bad enough his once flighty wife was now a single-minded businesswoman. Now he was starving too. But somewhere ahead, he saw a silver lining.

"Well, fine then. I'll swing by here in the mornings. That way you can fix my lunch and snack. I'll just pick it up. I'll eat dinner here too."

"No!" Mrs. Buchanan shook her head. "That's exactly the kind of thing we can't do. You're a married man. And don't forget the rough patch the two of you had a while back. This sort of thing must be settled between you and Daisy."

"But what if she never learns to cook or refuses to spend the money to hire a chef? It's bad enough that I have to iron my own shirts and darn my own socks. What if she makes me eat takeout Chinese every day for the next twenty years?" Tom heard his voice taking on an annoying, whiny quality, but he couldn't help it.

"Sweet Tommy." Mrs. Buchanan reached out to pat her baby boy's face. "These are things you need to discuss with Daisy. Tell her how you feel. I'll be happy to make out a list of all the food you like and how she should prepare it."

Tom sniffed and wiped his nose with his sleeve. He knew better. The power scales of their relationship had tipped in her favor. She made the money. She had ambition. She was growing a stock portfolio. The only thing he was growing was stubble on his unshaven face.

"I'm pretty sure she won't like that."

"Well," Mrs. Buchanan spoke slowly, phrasing her next thought carefully, "You know, I had to learn to cook when we had to let our chef go. I could teach you . . ."

"Good lord, Mom!" Tom yelped and jumped from the table. "I'm sure the situation won't warrant anything that extreme!"

Mentally, Tom could envision his friends at the club (Daisy gave him a small allowance so he could keep his membership) whipping him with towels and taunting, "Our wives have extra aprons, Tom, if you need them to loan you one with ruffles."

Mrs. Buchanan wrung her hands. "Oh dear. I didn't mean to upset you, sweetheart, but there are a lot of accomplished French chefs that are men."

"Yeah, that's because they're French!" Tom sulked, slumping in his chair and picking at his toast.

"Well, just talk with Daisy. Tell her your expectations now, before it's too late. Tell her you like pot roast on Monday nights, that you prefer your cheesecake made with organic cream, and be sure to remind her that you get diarrhea if you eat too much curry."

Tom nodded unhappily, his entire culinary world turned on its ear. He envisioned Daisy, her hair perfectly coifed as she walked briskly down Madison Avenue in her no-nonsense suit.

Tom sighed deeply and realized he was about to lose a lot of weight.

I stood in the kitchen as chilly winds rattled the window in the breakfast nook. Winter had come early to the South and a gust of dead leaves whipped across the backyard. I crossed my arms and eyed the ingredients on the counter. I'd laid them out in a neat row, trying to decide the best mode of attack. While most women view cooking as a leisurely, pleasurable activity . . . I don't. It's plain old warfare.

When Matt and I got married we made it through the ceremony (with my normally stoic mother crying loudly from her pew) and changed into our travel clothes before we left in a car emblazoned with shaving cream. On our way out of the church we stopped person to person, hugging and saying our goodbyes. An elderly man (who will remain anonymous) wished us well, before elbowing me and saying, "Well, sugar, I sure hope your mama taught you how to clean and cook!"

Matt spoke up quickly, "Actually, I like to cook."

The elderly man, who probably referred to the 1950s era of cigarettes and glass ceilings as "the good old days," was not to be deterred from making his point as he put his arm around me.

"Don't you dare make him do woman's work, ya hear?"

The three of us chuckled good-naturedly because back then I was naive and much nicer. If someone said that to me now I'd be hard pressed not to throw water on him after spraying him with lighter fluid and lighting a match.

The irony was I did know how to clean. Cleaning comes as naturally to me as riding a bike, memorizing all the dialogue from *Some Like It Hot,* and tweezing my eyebrows. It's a built-in component of my blood and heart. I smell bleach, and I smile. I get nervous, and I scrub the bathroom floor on my hands and knees. No problem.

But cooking, on the other hand, is an entirely different matter. It probably would have been fine had I married a good old boy, someone content to roar home in his truck, peel off his camouflaged jacket, and say, "Hey, what's for dinner? Chicken sticks and box mashed potatoes again? Hon, you're the best." But I didn't marry that guy. I married a foodie.

In this life, there are regular cooks and then there are foodies. The two categories are completely different, separated by a vast chasm that cannot be crossed (homemade macaroni and cheese on one side, guava paste on the other).

I can make meatloaf, grilled chicken, canned veggies accented by lovely bouillon cubes, and pudding mix pies. I can scramble eggs, make French toast in a skillet, and plop a pot roast in my Crock-Pot. I've mastered the fine art of not starving.

Matt, on the other hand, will come home with salmon, fresh dill, russet potatoes, and half a dozen spices I've never even heard of and say, "This looked fresh. I'm going to whip something up for dinner."

"Where are the directions? What recipe are you following?"

He'll shrug. "I'm just going to throw it all together and see what happens."

And what happens? It's delicious. It's food constructed with imagination, natural skill, and something foreign called "marinating."

As much as I considered myself a modern woman, and as much as I love eating delicious food cooked by a man with absolutely no sexist hang-ups, a part of me was bothered. After eight years of marriage, I secretly wondered if it made me less of a woman because I didn't know where the colander was stored in my own kitchen. Did it make me less feminine because I didn't have the foggiest idea how to run the food processor? Did I risk having my ovaries shrivel up and die because I ate nothing but takeout and sandwiches when Matt went out of town on business trips?

I mulled over these thoughts as the light dimmed outside, making me happy to be inside our cheerful kitchen with pale gray walls and white cabinets. Fine. Let Matt be an impressive foodie chef who served complicated Thai soups and Middle Eastern lamb stew with fresh ginger. I would become a baker. I would reclaim my femininity and take control of all things muffin-cake-pastry-tart-related. That way I could say, "Yeah, Matt fixes most of our meals, but I do all the baking."

And what better place to start than tackling my mother's homemade chocolate chip cookies? With great gusto I attacked my supplies of flour, sugar, brown sugar, butter, etc. (basically all the ingredients guaranteed to put a woman in elastic-waist pants in a matter of weeks).

I needed to recapture the castle, or in my case, the kitchen. I needed to measure up to the domestic cooking whiz I'd married.

Matt passed through the kitchen and kissed my forehead. "Looks like you're having a cookie marathon today."

"Yep," I said, determined to perfect my craft by nightfall.

Batch number one turned out beautifully. At least to the naked eye. Each cookie was round, fluffy, and golden with flecks of chocolate chips tempting even the most ardent dieter. I did a couple of Rockyesque victory punches in the privacy of the warm kitchen, smug at my clearly prodigy-like abilities.

"Mmmm, those look good!" Matt rounded the corner, grasped a spatula, and helped himself to one. I watched his face as he chewed, a funny, strange, tight expression stretching across his face.

"What? They're good, right?" I snatched up a cookie and plopped it in my mouth.

Matt and I stared at each other as we chewed. The cookies were bland and tasteless, barely sweet and slightly bitter. Their appearance promised lush, full cookie bliss. But these cookies were liars.

"What happened?" I began to yell, taking random bites out of every cookie. "They all taste awful!"

To Matt's credit, he never smiled, frowned, or gagged. He didn't even blink. "You might have used too much baking powder."

In a fit I emptied every cookie into the trash can and started over.

The second batch was an equal disaster. The cookies were comparable to a tiny propeller plane too weak to ever make it off the runway. They were paper thin, lifeless, and pitiful. In a fit, I grasped the spatula and tried to lift one from the cookie sheet. Instead, it merely wrinkled up like skin on a bulldog's face.

I shrieked, shoving the entire pan toward the back of the stove and throwing my apron to the ground. My face was covered in flour, every mixing bowl in the house was dirty, and the air taunted me with the aroma of baked goods. But there were no baked goods. There was just me, my mother's impossible cookie recipe, and a husband hiding somewhere in the dark recesses of the house, too scared to come out.

"Fine," I said to myself like one of those mentally unbalanced people who wander the streets around office buildings. "Stupid cookies. I don't need to prove anything. This is so stupid. This is ridiculous."

To regain my sanity, I decided I needed a long bath with candles and a good book. As I drifted beneath the bubbles I tried to ignore the nagging feeling that I'd failed as a female. I railed at the idea that cleaning or cooking was "woman's work," just as holding down a job was just "man's work." And yet, the cliché had at some point stuck to me like a bloodsucking leech, draining my confidence and planting a seed of paranoia that my ovaries were linked to my ability to bake cookies.

As I soaked, I thought about Angela. I thought about the summer that had flown past, filled with hospital stays and surgery. I thought about the fall that had passed even faster, a blur of falling leaves and more doctor visits. More bad news. I thought about what she was going through just a few miles away. I'd been at her house almost every day that week. I sat with her while she watched TV. I took out the trash. I sat some more. The waiting was agony. There was nothing left to be done.

The truth was I'd stayed home to make cookies and hide in my house instead of visiting her again. I felt guilty that I needed a break from worry and grief when she was afforded none. She couldn't escape what was happening.

I dried off, wrapped myself in a cozy robe, and lay in bed, trying to read Erma Bombeck. Erma is my favorite and can usually cheer me out of any funk. But she wasn't working this time. I snorted under my breath.

"I bet Erma never made cookies that tasted like the bitter spray I put on Mabel's legs to keep her from biting herself."

The clock ticked, and I stewed. At some point Matt brought me a glass of water and patted my head.

"You should really try and get some sleep. Maybe you should take something?"

I shook my head. "I'm fine."

"Do you want to talk about it? How is she?"

"No, I don't want to talk about Angela!"

I wasn't sure if my emotions were coming or going, but these strange bursts of anger were more and more common as the weeks passed. But when I looked into his eyes, my heart softened.

"I'm sorry to be such a handful."

"That's okay. It's been bad lately." Matt kissed my forehead and left the room, gently closing the door behind him.

And as I lay there at 11:30 at night, the dog next door began to bark. Again.

I'm normally very tolerant of belligerent, rude, small dogs. After all, I own one. But after watching the clock for forty-three minutes as the barking continued, at 12:13 I blew a fuse.

The entire world was asleep, and it was just me and that dog. Me, with my failed cookie-making abilities, and the dog, with his failed brain that obviously lacked the "shut up or one of the neighbors might shoot me with a BB gun" switch. I decided it was time the two of us looked each other in the eye.

On my way out, I remembered the slender black cylinder of mace hanging from my key ring. In a fit of insomnia, I grabbed it. I'd shut that dog up if it was the last thing I did. I passed by Mabel and Matt, who had fallen asleep on the couch watching the Food Network. Of course.

The back door banged open and I flipped on the floodlights. There he stood. A ten pound ball of black fur with a mouth and teeth like the alien Sigourney Weaver nurtured. He was momentarily stunned into silence, but upon gaining a second wind of insane barking energy, he opened his mouth and began to sound the alarm once more.

"Hey! Mini Cujo!" I was hunched over and creeping toward him like a crazy woman. "What's your problem, huh?"

The dog continued its high-pitched girlish barking, reminding me momentarily of the time Rebecca chased me around the house, pinching the thin skin on the back of my arms as I tried to run and simultaneously slap behind me.

And as I stood there, mace in one hand, full moon above, cold wind whipping my hair, the realization of what was really happening set in.

Things were bad. The truth was my sudden mania over cooking was just a symptom of the tornado in my head. My heart was hurting. Angela was sick. Very sick.

For anyone who has borne witness to the depths of cancer, the dark shadows that draw over a room, a life, a family . . . it needs no explanation. And while I'd been task-oriented as Angela's helper and friend, I hadn't known that the ravages of cancer almost always reach a certain crescendo. Suddenly there's nothing left to do but wait and see what happens.

I wasn't very good at waiting. I desperately needed something to do; I needed a project that would turn out okay and be successful. I needed those cookies to be the greatest cookies in the world, to remind me that miracles were still possible. After all, if I—the woman who accidentally burned chicken noodle soup and ruined instant mix muffins—could bake a tasty batch of my mother's perfect cookies . . . surely Angela could be miraculously healed of cancer.

I whirled and returned to the house, heading straight for the wrinkled cookies still sitting atop the stove. Carefully, I cut the chocolate chips out and crumbled a handful of the dry disaster into my palm and returned to the backyard.

Mini Cujo was at this point thoroughly freaked out by my presence. And why wouldn't he be? After all, he was merely trying to howl at the moon when I appeared like a dark-eyed zombie. He paced the fence, shrieking. No doubt he feared being eaten, boiled, or thrown against the nearest tree. What he should have feared was the mace, but no one ever said that the original Cujo or his descendants possessed above average intelligence.

I knelt beside the fence. "Did you know I can't even bake chocolate chip cookies?"

Mini Cujo scaled back his screaming to a subtle growl and stood closer, his little eyes bugged and wary. Carefully, he lapped his tongue through the fence, taking a cookie crumb from my hand. His small butt began to vibrate back and forth as his stub of a tail worked the air like a gleeful propeller.

And that's when I realized Mini Cujo and I had quite a bit in common. There he was, alone, underweight, afraid in the dark, and yet desperately trying to prove himself with excessive barking. There I was, nearing thirty with no distinguishable domestic skills other than scouring floors with bleach, trying my best to jump through the greatest Olympic Betty Crocker Hoop—Mom's homemade cookies—in some kind of backward attempt to prove my friend would live. It didn't make sense. But then again, it did.

And as I crouched in the moonlight, feeding my new friend tiny pieces of cookie to get him to shut up, I realized not all of us are meant for the same things. Some dogs are graceful German shepherds who ride in patrol cars and protect the peace, while others are fat shar-peis who have difficulty cleaning the cracks in their own faces. Some people are born to be great domestic cooks, flipping pancakes, sautéing things, adding a dash and a pinch of this and that, and making great cookies from scratch. And others of us are meant to perform tricky driving techniques during rush hour traffic, to pick up Chinese takeout, and, if we're lucky, marry someone who will keep us from starving.

As I sat with the little dog, I told him about Angela. He lapped tiny treats from my hand as I explained to him about hospice. I unloaded onto Mini Cujo all the things I didn't like to talk about. Big hot tears ran down my cheeks as a cold breeze blew leaves across the yard. I crouched near the freezing ground and told the little dog about how Angela's husband Bryan made sure she had her favorite lip gloss on the bedside table at all times. He shaved her legs, carried her to the couch, and changed her clothes. I explained how when I visited Angela we laid in bed together and I hummed songs.

Despite the drugs, she cracked a joke saying, "Liz, we're going to have to get a pitch pipe in here if you persist in this amateur singing career." Then she cleared her throat and asked seriously, "How is your progress in the library? Are you getting a lot of writing done?"

She asked this question more and more often, prodding me constantly about a book I was working on.

"Fine," I lied.

"Listen to me," she stared at me intently. "You keep writing. It puts the light behind your eyes. And for heaven's sake, remember it's a library, not an office."

"Okay, deal." I nodded, swallowing my sobs down furiously, determined not to cry in front of her.

"Don't look at me like that," she commanded, adjusting her oxygen tube.

I reached out and held her hand. Usually she squeezed my hand and then pushed me away. This time she held on.

And when she could talk no more, she reached out to pet her dog Sabi who refused to leave her side.

I'd prayed more and more in the previous months. The prayers that had started outside the hospital, angry and lightning bolt–worthy, changed. I cried to God. I sat and talked with him for hours, telling him about the horrible things happening to my friend. I asked him for mercy. I asked him for healing. And in the last few days, I'd started asking for something simpler. I asked for her not to suffer anymore.

And I prayed there underneath the moon as the dead leaves swirled in the wind. I prayed as Mini Cujo and I sat together. God didn't speak to me. I didn't see a vision or a sign. But I knew He was there. I knew He was listening. And I knew what He wanted from me. I was supposed to be grateful. He couldn't have picked a harder request.

I fed one last cookie to Mini Cujo. One thing was certain, I was grateful for the little dog's company. It was a fair trade-off after all. He ate tiny pieces of my bad cookies and I told him all the things hurting my heart. I needed a shoulder to lean on, and Mini Cujo had no frame of reference for homemade chocolate chip cookies. He merely wagged his tail with gusto, proclaiming me the queen of cookies, and for the first time in months, a weight lifted.

CHAPTER 14

A Dream in December

Her chest rose and fell in shallow, inconspicuous breaths. I reached out to touch her long, cold fingers, clasping them, wishing I could transfer my warmth to her. Transfer a little life to her.

With the cancer came the drugs. They were necessary to keep away the pain. But with the drugs, we lost her. She slipped further and further away, fading before our very eyes. No more talking. No more eating. No more Angela. I was losing my friend.

And quickly, simply, she was awake. Long lashes blinked over green eyes, her pupils alert and focused. She smiled, beamed, sparkled, and made my heart leap within my chest.

Snow White awoke in her glass coffin.

She drew a deep, strong breath and slowly removed the oxygen from her face. She didn't need it anymore. She pushed herself upright in bed as I watched, as my mouth fell open, as tingles ran up my arms.

She drew another breath and stared directly at me, smiling. "Hi."

"Oh, Ang." The words burst from my mouth, hurrying to catch her, hurrying in case she fell back asleep. "I'm so very proud of you."

Her smile turned shy, embarrassed. "Really?"

"Yes," I gushed, tears streaming down my face as I realized I had a chance to tell her things, that it wasn't too late. "This is so horrible, and you're so very strong. I'm proud of you. And I love you."

She smiled wider, her beautiful face awake and pain-free, dark hair regrown and flowing on her shoulders. She was healed. She was new again.

"Thank you. I love you too," she said, the shy smile still in place.

And then I woke up. The chill still on my arms, her voice and words just inside my ears. Inside my heart. And I knew her pain was done. And I knew her suffering was gone.

I got out of bed in the predawn darkness of a cold December day. The sky was the darkest midnight blue, the air filled with icicles and silence. I began to walk laps around the house, careful to avoid certain creaking floorboards. I waited for the phone call I knew would come, the phone call that would tell me she was gone.

As I walked from room to room I began to mentally catalogue everything. I catalogued my dream, so I would never forget. I noted the pile of clean clothes waiting to be folded in the corner of the living room. I observed the bookshelves in my library stacked with un-alphabetized authors and rocks from past vacations. I looked at the black-and-white family photos lining the hallway, faces of people long gone smiling down on me, assuring me that there was much more to this life than I could see with my eyes.

I noted the dust bunnies in the guest room, the giant Mabel-nose smudges on the front window where she routinely mashed her face and threatened the neighborhood squirrels. And finally, after much walking, I ended up on the back patio. I sat on the steps, steps that needed to be swept, and looked up at the sky. Distant white stars were fading, a sliver of silvery moon slipped away just over the roofline of the house.

At any other time in my life I would have rolled up my sleeves and thrown myself headlong into cleaning. I would have washed dishes, terminated the dust bunnies, and rapidly folded clothes, putting my tiny universe into order. I would have worked until I was too tired to cry.

But that morning I didn't clean. I was grateful for the unswept floors, the overflowing bookshelves. I was grateful for my husband who was snoring so loudly I could hear it outside. I was grateful for my mixed breed schnauzer ramming her nose into my leg when she needed attention, like a demented hairy little porpoise. I was grateful to be a part of it, grateful to be alive. Grateful to sit on the steps, sucking the cold winter air into my lungs. And somehow in the middle of the freezing tears that slid down my cheeks, I was oh so grateful to God. Grateful for Angela. Grateful to know what it was like to have found a kindred spirit.

It was at that moment, underneath a freezing December dawn sky, I decided to be grateful for the rest of my life. I decided to stop flushing with embarrassment when guests noticed Mabel's drool rings on the couch cushions, because this is my life. The leaky roof, the dated fixtures, and the sleepwalking husband who gives me wedgies. And within this life there will always be estate sale battles and plumbing disasters.

There will always be a broken DVD player, a pile of shoes in the living room, and batches of awful homemade cookies.

But there are also days spent frolicking in the snow with Mabel. There are long evening walks with Matt, Doris Day movie marathons, and afternoons spent reading as the sun creates shadowed spiderweb patterns on the wooden floors.

I believe that if my fictional friends found themselves thrust from the pages of their books and into the cold light of reality, their stories really would look just like ours. Anne's children would throw a fit in church and then scream dramatically within earshot of other parishioners, "No, please Mom, don't spank me!" Scarlett and Rhett would have ended up in couples counseling, and Nancy Drew's normally plucky attitude would have deflated like an old balloon as she watched her newly installed dining room chandelier crash to the floor because Ned bypassed reading the directions and didn't drill it to the ceiling properly.

They would look just like us because in reality, there is no such thing as perfection. There is no perfect house, spouse, pet, or holiday tradition. There are flaws in everything. But in embracing those flaws, we become thankful. And eventually, thankful turns into grateful. And grateful, well, gratefulness turns into happiness.

My entire life my mother has been consistent. She has always painted. She has always loved the movie *Rose Marie,* even when my sisters and I made fun of Nelson Eddy and sang mockingly, mimicking his dorky Canadian Mounties uniform while we stuffed small pillows into the sides of our jogging pants. And whenever Mom spied the wrinkle between my eyebrows, always a telltale sign of distress, she'd say, "Have you prayed about it?"

And as I sat looking up at the pale morning sky and the dimming stars, I heard Mom's question again.

"Have you prayed about it?"

I smoothed the wrinkle between my eyebrows, wiped away my tears, and smiled. I smiled because at that moment, I didn't need to. I didn't need to pray because God was right there next to me on those cold steps. His arm was around me and we gazed up at the icy dawn together. I was with him and so was Angela.

Epilogue

I suppose the big question is: Do I understand? Do I understand any more now than the first day Angela found the lump in her arm? Do I have any great wisdom on suffering? Why it happened? Why she's gone? Honestly, there are times when it feels like I know as little today as I did when it all began.

A good friend once advised me, "People don't want to be told how 'it' is; they want to hear what 'it' was like." And that's really all anyone can do. I can only tell you what it was like for me to watch a friend die. But what I have come to understand is that God never leaves us. He is not the leader of an exclusive club or an absentee clockmaker that sits back and waits for this all to be over. God is faithful, and he takes us home.

I don't know how this story ends for me. I wonder how it will feel to die, to cross the unknown into a world that is unimaginable to my human mind. I wonder what I'll see, what I'll look like, if I'll be able to fly. Everyone says there's a mansion involved. I'd be lying if I said I wasn't holding my breath on that one. Fingers crossed God gives me a white farmhouse with a green roof instead of a McMansion. After all, I'm not a fan of open floor plans.

I do know that God will be there, smiling, as he opens the door and Angela asks if I'd like tea with cream or sugar. Knowing her, she'll probably have unpacked and organized the new library, alphabetizing all my favorite books, all those familiar and beloved characters. Perhaps we'll invite Jane Austen for tea or go fishing with Louisa May Alcott.

And I hope that then, in my new home where I'll have tea with Angela, I'll understand God's plan. I hope to stand before him like a child and say, "Why did she suffer?" But even more than that, I hope that once I'm there, I won't even feel the need to ask. Hopefully I'll smile, nod my head, and just know.

Angela's death was a gradual descent. My life, by that same token, shifted onto an irreversible course change. She died, I lived. Her friendship helped me overcome my dissatisfaction and discontentment. Because of the journey with her, I gave up my unrealistic expectations about hearth and home.

There is much happiness in a successful dinner party, a lushly planted garden, and finding a free buffet table on the curb. But when the quest to transform our domestic realities into an unattainable level of perfection becomes a lifestyle, that's where we lose our joy. Domestic reality is salty and sweet, irritating and comforting, sad and funny. But above all, we have to learn to live it without ladders to climb, without levels of perfection to attain; to throw away the shame that comes with perceived imperfections. In short, we need to allow ourselves to simply be blessed.

On his eightieth birthday, Hoagy Carmichael said, "I'm a bit disappointed in myself. I know I could have accomplished a hell of a lot more . . . I could write anything any time I wanted to. But I let other things get in the way . . . I've been floating around in the breeze."

Before my friendship with Angela, I was floating. I'm not floating anymore.

She came into my life at a time when I was dissatisfied with my house, my ability to cook, my yard, and my job. But my experience with her, along with the crazy challenges of domestic life, changed my outlook. I stopped trying to control my own personal Green Gables kingdom and instead tried to develop the joy inside me, which has nothing to do with acquiring or cleaning or renovating. Somewhere in this process I turned to face God, something I had managed to avoid most of my life.

Angela gave me back my joy, my freedom, and in some indefinable way played matchmaker between me and the God who was with us all the time. I accept that gift. I am truly, finally, grateful. After all, she was right. The universe doesn't care whether my kitchen is clean. No one stole my Green Gables. Beneath the dirty clothes piles, leaky roof, and literary friends . . . it was there all the time.

About the Author

Elizabeth Owen began her writing career at age seven when she penned in her diary, "My letle seester makes me cruzy." She authors the popular *Mabel's House* blog (http://mabels house.blogspot.com/) about life in Little Rock with her husband, Matt, daughter, Jane, and dog, Mabel. *Mabel's House* has been featured several times on *Apartment Therapy* and *Design Sponge*. Elizabeth's articles and projects have appeared in *At Home in Arkansas* and *Better Homes and Gardens*.

Elizabeth spends her free time spray-painting curbside furniture finds and fixing up her 1950s ranch home. She graduated from Harding University in 2002 with an English literature degree and works at the University of Arkansas at Little Rock. *My (not so) Storybook Life* is her first book.